MznLnx

Missing Links Exam Preps

Exam Prep for

New Venture Management: The Entrepreneur's Roadmap

Kuratko & Hornsby, 1st Edition

The MznLnx Exam Prep is your link from the texbook and lecture to your exams.
The MznLnx Exam Preps are unauthorized and comprehensive reviews of your textbooks.

All material provided by MznLnx and Rico Publications (c) 2010
Textbook publishers and textbook authors do not particpate in or contribute to these reviews.

MznLnx

Rico Publications

Exam Prep for New Venture Management: The Entrepreneur's Roadmap
1st Edition
Kuratko & Hornsby

Publisher: Raymond Houge
Assistant Editor: Michael Rouger
Text and Cover Designer: Lisa Buckner
Marketing Manager: Sara Swagger
Project Manager, Editorial Production: Jerry Emerson
Art Director: Vernon Lowerui

Product Manager: Dave Mason
Editorial Assitant: Rachel Guzmanji
Pedagogy: Debra Long
Cover Image: Jim Reed/Getty Images
Text and Cover Printer: City Printing, Inc.
Compositor: Media Mix, Inc.

(c) 2010 Rico Publications
ALL RIGHTS RESERVED. No part of this work
covered by the copyright may be reproduced or
used in any form or by an means--graphic, electronic,
or mechanical, including photocopying, recording,
taping, Web distribution, information storage, and
retrieval systems, or in any other manner--without the
written permission of the publisher.

Printed in the United States
ISBN:

For more information about our products, contact us at:
Dave.Mason@RicoPublications.com

For permission to use material from this text or
product, submit a request online to:
Dave.Mason@RicoPublications.com

Contents

CHAPTER 1
New Ventures: The Quiet Giant — 1

CHAPTER 2
New or Acquired Ventures: The Pathways — 5

CHAPTER 3
Franchising: The Hybrid — 11

CHAPTER 4
Successful Business Plans: The Roadmap — 16

CHAPTER 5
Legal Forms of Ventures: The Structure — 20

CHAPTER 6
Market Research: The Niche — 25

CHAPTER 7
Strategic Pricing: The Hook — 32

CHAPTER 8
Start-Up Capital: The Injection — 38

CHAPTER 9
Financial Statements: The Scorecard — 45

CHAPTER 10
Financial Analysis: The Gauges — 52

CHAPTER 11
Human Resources: The People — 57

CHAPTER 12
Growing Ventures: The Future — 67

ANSWER KEY — 78

TO THE STUDENT

COMPREHENSIVE

The *MznLnx* Exam Prep series is designed to help you pass your exams. Editors at MznLnx review your textbooks and then prepare these practice exams to help you master the textbook material. Unlike study guides, workbooks, and practice tests provided by the texbook publisher and textbook authors, *MznLnx* gives you **all** of the material in each chapter in exam form, not just samples, so you can be sure to nail your exam.

MECHANICAL

The MznLnx Exam Prep series creates exams that will help you learn the subject matter as well as test you on your understanding. Each question is designed to help you master the concept. Just working through the exams, you gain an understanding of the subject--its a simple mechanical process that produces success.

INTEGRATED STUDY GUIDE AND REVIEW

MznLnx is not just a set of exams designed to test you, its also a comprehensive review of the subject content. Each exam question is also a review of the concept, making sure that you will get the answer correct without having to go to other sources of material. You learn as you go! Its the easiest way to pass an exam.

HUMOR

Studying can be tedious and dry. MznLnx's instructional design includes moderate humor within the exam questions on occassion, to break the tedium and revitalize the brain

Chapter 1. New Ventures: The Quiet Giant

1. An _____ is a person who has possession of an enterprise and assumes significant accountability for the inherent risks and the outcome. It is an ambitious leader who combines land, labor, and capital to create and market new goods or services. The term is a loanword from French and was first defined by the Irish economist Richard Cantillon.
   a. Entrepreneur
   b. A Stake in the Outcome
   c. AAAI
   d. A4e

2. _____ according to Onuoha (2007) is the practice of starting new organizations or revitalizing mature organizations, particularly new businesses generally in response to identified opportunities. _____ is often a difficult undertaking, as a vast majority of new businesses fail. Entrepreneurial activities are substantially different depending on the type of organization that is being started.
   a. Entrepreneurship
   b. AAAI
   c. A4e
   d. A Stake in the Outcome

3. A _____ is a business that is privately owned and operated, with a small number of employees and relatively low volume of sales. The legal definition of 'small' often varies by country and industry, but is generally under 100 employees in the United States and under 50 employees in the European Union. In comparison, the definition of mid-sized business by the number of employees is generally under 500 in the U.S. and 250 for the European Union.
   a. Golden Boot Compensation
   b. Pre-determined overhead rate
   c. Critical Success Factor
   d. Small business

4. _____s are expenses that change in proportion to the activity of a business. In other words, _____ is the sum of marginal costs. It can also be considered normal costs.
   a. Cost accounting
   b. Fixed costs
   c. Cost overrun
   d. Variable cost

5. In economics, business, retail, and accounting, a _____ is the value of money that has been used up to produce something, and hence is not available for use anymore. In economics, a _____ is an alternative that is given up as a result of a decision. In business, the _____ may be one of acquisition, in which case the amount of money expended to acquire it is counted as _____.

Chapter 1. New Ventures: The Quiet Giant

   a. Cost
   b. Cost allocation
   c. Cost overrun
   d. Fixed costs

6. In economics, _____ is a rise in the general level of prices of goods and services in an economy over a period of time. When the general price level rises, each unit of the functional currency buys fewer goods and services; consequently, _____ is a decline in the real value of money--a loss of purchasing power in the internal medium of exchange which is also the monetary unit of account in an economy. A chief measure of general price-level _____ is the general _____ rate, which is the percentage change in a general price index (normally the Consumer Price Index) over time.
   a. Economy
   b. A Stake in the Outcome
   c. A4e
   d. Inflation

7. An _____ or stagiaire is one who works in a temporary position with an emphasis on on-the-job training rather than merely employment, making it similar to an apprenticeship. _____s are usually college or university students, but they can also be high school students or post graduate adults seeking skills for a new career. Student _____ships provide opportunities for students to gain experience in their field, determine if they have an interest in a particular career, create a network of contacts, or gain school credit.
   a. Employee handbook
   b. Intern
   c. Employment
   d. Underemployment

8. In economics, _____ is the desire to own something and the ability to pay for it. The term _____ signifies the ability or the willingness to buy a particular commodity at a given point of time.
   a. 1990 Clean Air Act
   b. 28-hour day
   c. 33 Strategies of War
   d. Demand

9. _____ refers to the process of screening, and selecting qualified people for a job at an organization or firm mid- and large-size organizations and companies often retain professional recruiters or outsource some of the process to _____ agencies. External _____ is the process of attracting and selecting employees from outside the organization.

The _____ industry has four main types of agencies: employment agencies, _____ websites and job search engines, 'headhunters' for executive and professional _____, and in-house _____.

a. Recruitment
b. Referral recruitment
c. Labour hire
d. Recruitment Process Outsourcing

10. _____ is the self-government of a nation, country or some portion thereof, generally exercising sovereignty.

The term _____ is used in contrast to subjugation, which refers to a region as a 'territory' --subject to the political and military control of an external government. The word is sometimes used in a weaker sense to contrast with hegemony, the indirect control of one nation by another, more powerful nation.

a. A4e
b. AAAI
c. A Stake in the Outcome
d. Independence

11. _____ is the probability that an individual will keep his or her job; a job with a high level of _____ is such that a person with the job would have a small chance of becoming unemployed.

_____ is dependent on economy, prevailing business conditions, and the individual's personal skills. It has been found that people have more _____ in times of economic expansion and less in times of a recession.

a. Job security
b. Just cause
c. Multiple careers
d. Hygiene factors

12. _____ is a contract between two parties, one being the employer and the other being the employee. An employee may be defined as: 'A person in the service of another under any contract of hire, express or implied, oral or written, where the employer has the power or right to control and direct the employee in the material details of how the work is to be performed.' Black's Law Dictionary page 471 (5th ed. 1979.)

a. Employment rate
b. Exit interview
c. Employment counsellor
d. Employment

13. A _____ is a process in which a potential employee is evaluated by an employer for prospective employment in their company, organization and was established in the late 16th century.

A _____ typically precedes the hiring decision, and is used to evaluate the candidate. The interview is usually preceded by the evaluation of submitted résumés from interested candidates, then selecting a small number of candidates for interviews.

a. Payrolling
b. Job interview
c. Split shift
d. Supported employment

14. _____ is a legally declared inability or impairment of ability of an individual or organization to pay its creditors. Creditors may file a _____ petition against a debtor ('involuntary _____') in an effort to recoup a portion of what they are owed or initiate a restructuring. In the majority of cases, however, _____ is initiated by the debtor (a 'voluntary _____' that is filed by the insolvent individual or organization.)

a. 28-hour day
b. 33 Strategies of War
c. Bankruptcy
d. 1990 Clean Air Act

15. A _____ is a documented investigation of a Market that is used to inform a firm's planning activities particularly around decision of: inventory, purchase, work force expansion/contraction, facility expansion, purchases of capital equipment, promotional activities, and many other aspects of a company.

Not all managers are asked to conduct a _____, but all managers must make decisions using _____ data and understand how the data was derived. So all managers need a reasonable understanding of the tools most used for making sales forecasts and analyzing markets.

a. 1990 Clean Air Act
b. Marketing research process
c. Marketing research
d. Market analysis

Chapter 2. New or Acquired Ventures: The Pathways

1. In business, _____ is the total liabilities minus total outside assets of an individual or a company. For a company, this is called shareholders' preference and may be referred to as book value. _____ is stated as at a particular year in time.
   a. Novated lease
   b. Deferred compensation
   c. Payback period
   d. Net worth

2. An _____ is a person who has possession of an enterprise and assumes significant accountability for the inherent risks and the outcome. It is an ambitious leader who combines land, labor, and capital to create and market new goods or services. The term is a loanword from French and was first defined by the Irish economist Richard Cantillon.
   a. AAAI
   b. A Stake in the Outcome
   c. A4e
   d. Entrepreneur

3. A _____ is a formal statement of a set of business goals, the reasons why they are believed attainable, and the plan for reaching those goals. It may also contain background information about the organization or team attempting to reach those goals.

   The business goals may be defined for for-profit or for non-profit organizations.

   a. Distributed management
   b. Time management
   c. Crisis management
   d. Business plan

4. A _____ is a documented investigation of a Market that is used to inform a firm's planning activities particularly around decision of: inventory, purchase, work force expansion/contraction, facility expansion, purchases of capital equipment, promotional activities, and many other aspects of a company.

   Not all managers are asked to conduct a _____, but all managers must make decisions using _____ data and understand how the data was derived. So all managers need a reasonable understanding of the tools most used for making sales forecasts and analyzing markets.

   a. Market analysis
   b. Marketing research process
   c. Marketing research
   d. 1990 Clean Air Act

Chapter 2. New or Acquired Ventures: The Pathways

5. _____ refers to bodies of techniques for investigating phenomena, acquiring new knowledge, or correcting and integrating previous knowledge. To be termed scientific, a method of inquiry must be based on gathering observable, empirical and measurable evidence subject to specific principles of reasoning. A _____ consists of the collection of data through observation and experimentation, and the formulation and testing of hypotheses.

   a. 1990 Clean Air Act
   b. Scientific method
   c. 33 Strategies of War
   d. 28-hour day

6. The term '_____' refers to the concept of collecting information and attempting to spot a pattern in the information. In some fields of study, the term '_____' has more formally-defined meanings.

In project management _____ is a mathematical technique that uses historical results to predict future outcome.

   a. Least squares
   b. Trend analysis
   c. Stepwise regression
   d. Regression analysis

7. _____ is a broad label that refers to any individuals or households that use goods and services generated within the economy. The concept of a _____ is used in different contexts, so that the usage and significance of the term may vary.

Typically when business people and economists talk of _____s they are talking about person as _____, an aggregated commodity item with little individuality other than that expressed in the buy/not-buy decision.

   a. 28-hour day
   b. 1990 Clean Air Act
   c. 33 Strategies of War
   d. Consumer

8. _____ is the number of goods/services that can be purchased with a unit of currency. For example, if you had taken one dollar to a store in the 1950s, you would have been able to buy a greater number of items than you would today, indicating that you would have had a greater _____ in the 1950s. Currency can be either a commodity money, like gold or silver, or fiat currency like US dollars.

a. Purchasing power
b. 33 Strategies of War
c. 1990 Clean Air Act
d. 28-hour day

9. _____ refers to an assessment of the viability, stability and profitability of a business, sub-business or project.

It is performed by professionals who prepare reports using ratios that make use of information taken from financial statements and other reports. These reports are usually presented to top management as one of their bases in making business decisions.

a. 1990 Clean Air Act
b. 33 Strategies of War
c. Financial analysis
d. 28-hour day

10. _____ is an integrated communications-based process through which individuals and communities discover that existing and newly-identified needs and wants may be satisfied by the products and services of others.

_____ is defined by the American _____ Association as the activity, set of institutions, and processes for creating, communicating, delivering, and exchanging offerings that have value for customers, clients, partners, and society at large. The term developed from the original meaning which referred literally to going to market, as in shopping, or going to a market to buy or sell goods or services.

a. Disruptive technology
b. Customer relationship management
c. Marketing
d. Market development

11. In decision theory and estimation theory, the _____ of an estimator, $\hat{\theta}$, of an unknown parameter of the distribution, θ, is the expected value of the loss function

$$R(\theta, \hat{\theta}) = \mathbb{E}_\theta L(\theta, \hat{\theta}) = \int L(\theta, \hat{\theta})\, dP_\theta.$$

where dP_θ is a probability measure parametrized by θ.

- For a scalar parameter θ and a quadratic loss function,

$$L(\theta, \hat{\theta}) = (\theta - \hat{\theta})^2$$

the _____ function becomes the mean squared error of the estimate,

$$R(\theta, \hat{\theta}) = E_\theta(\theta - \hat{\theta})^2$$

- In density estimation, the unknown parameter is probability density itself. The loss function is typically chosen to be a norm in an appropriate function space. For example, for L^2 norm,

$$L(f, \hat{f}) = \|f - \hat{f}\|_2^2$$

the _____ function becomes the mean integrated squared error

$$R(f, \hat{f}) = E\|f - \hat{f}\|^2$$

   a. Linear model
   b. Financial modeling
   c. Risk
   d. Risk aversion

12. _____ is the set of tasks, knowledge, and techniques required to identify business needs and determine solutions to business problems. Solutions often include a systems development component, but may also consist of process improvement or organizational change. The person who carries out this task is called a business analyst or _____.
   a. 28-hour day
   b. Door-to-door selling
   c. Business analysis
   d. 1990 Clean Air Act

13. In business and accounting, _____s are everything of value that is owned by a person or company. Any property or object of value that one possesses, usually considered as applicable to the payment of one's debts is considered an _____. Simplistically stated, _____s are things of value that can be readily converted into cash.

Chapter 2. New or Acquired Ventures: The Pathways

a. A Stake in the Outcome
b. AAAI
c. Asset
d. A4e

14. In law, _____ refers to the process by which a company (or part of a company) is brought to an end, and the assets and property of the company redistributed. _____ can also be referred to as winding-up or dissolution, although dissolution technically refers to the last stage of _____. The process of _____ also arises when customs, an authority or agency in a country responsible for collecting and safeguarding customs duties, determines the final computation or ascertainment of the duties or drawback accruing on an entry.

a. 33 Strategies of War
b. Liquidation
c. 1990 Clean Air Act
d. 28-hour day

15. _____ is the value on a given date of a future payment or series of future payments, discounted to reflect the time value of money and other factors such as investment risk. _____ calculations are widely used in business and economics to provide a means to compare cash flows at different times on a meaningful 'like to like' basis.

If offered a choice between $100 today or $100 in one year, everyone will choose $100 today.

a. Net present value
b. Present value
c. 1990 Clean Air Act
d. Discounted cash flow

16. _____ refers to the movement of cash into or out of a business or financial product. It is usually measured during a specified, finite period of time. Measurement of _____ can be used

- to determine a project's rate of return or value. The time of _____s into and out of projects are used as inputs in financial models such as internal rate of return, and net present value.
- to determine problems with a business's liquidity. Being profitable does not necessarily mean being liquid. A company can fail because of a shortage of cash, even while profitable.
- as an alternate measure of a business's profits when it is believed that accrual accounting concepts do not represent economic realities. For example, a company may be notionally profitable but generating little operational cash (as may be the case for a company that barters its products rather than selling for cash.) In such a case, the company may be deriving additional operating cash by issuing shares evaluating default risk, re-investment requirements, etc.

_____ is a generic term used differently depending on the context. It may be defined by users for their own purposes.

a. Cash flow
b. Gross profit
c. Gross profit margin
d. Sweat equity

17. _____ is one of a series of accounting transactions dealing with the billing of customers who owe money to a person, company or organization for goods and services that have been provided to the customer. In most business entities this is typically done by generating an invoice and mailing or electronically delivering it to the customer, who in turn must pay it within an established timeframe called credit or payment terms.

An example of a common payment term is Net 30, meaning payment is due in the amount of the invoice 30 days from the date of invoice.

a. Accounts receivable
b. Other revenue
c. Accumulated Depreciation
d. A Stake in the Outcome

Chapter 3. Franchising: The Hybrid

1. _____ refers to the methods of practicing and using another person's business philosophy. The franchisor grants the independent operator the right to distribute its products, techniques, and trademarks for a percentage of gross monthly sales and a royalty fee. Various tangibles and intangibles such as national or international advertising, training, and other support services are commonly made available by the franchisor.
    a. ServiceMaster
    b. 1990 Clean Air Act
    c. 28-hour day
    d. Franchising

2. _____ is the state or fact of exclusive rights and control over property, which may be an object, land/real estate or intellectual property. An _____ right is also referred to as title. The concept of _____ has existed for thousands of years and in all cultures.
    a. Emanation of the state
    b. A Stake in the Outcome
    c. A4e
    d. Ownership

3. The _____ is an independent agency of the United States government, established in 1914 by the _____ Act. Its principal mission is the promotion of 'consumer protection' and the elimination and prevention of what regulators perceive to be harmfully 'anti-competitive' business practices, such as coercive monopoly.

    The _____ Act was one of President Wilson's major acts against trusts.

    a. 33 Strategies of War
    b. 28-hour day
    c. 1990 Clean Air Act
    d. Federal Trade Commission

4. A _____ is a name or trademark connected with a product or producer. _____s have become increasingly important components of culture and the economy, now being described as 'cultural accessories and personal philosophies'.

    Some people distinguish the psychological aspect of a _____ from the experiential aspect.

    a. Brand loyalty
    b. Brand extension
    c. Brand
    d. Brand awareness

Chapter 3. Franchising: The Hybrid

5. Descriptive _____ assist in describing the distinguishable selling point(s) of the product to the customer (eg Snap Crackle ' Pop or Bitter Lemon.)

Associative _____ provide the customer with an associated word for what the product promises to do or be (e.g. Walkman, Sensodyne or Natrel)

Finally, Freestanding _____ have no links or ties to either descriptions or associations of use. (eg Mars Bar or Pantene)

The act of associating a product or service with a brand has become part of pop culture.

   a. Brand names
   b. Brand image
   c. Brand awareness
   d. Brand extension

6. In economics, business, retail, and accounting, a _____ is the value of money that has been used up to produce something, and hence is not available for use anymore. In economics, a _____ is an alternative that is given up as a result of a decision. In business, the _____ may be one of acquisition, in which case the amount of money expended to acquire it is counted as _____.
   a. Cost allocation
   b. Fixed costs
   c. Cost overrun
   d. Cost

7. _____ is a term used in the stock-trading world to describe the practice of buying shares or other securities without actually having the capital to cover the trade. This is possible when recently bought or sold shares are unsettled, and therefore have not been paid for.

Since stock transactions usually settle after three business days, a crafty trader can buy a stock and sell it the following day, without ever having sufficient funds in the account.

   a. Stockholder
   b. Shareholder
   c. 1990 Clean Air Act
   d. Free riding

Chapter 3. Franchising: The Hybrid

8. A _____ is a business that is privately owned and operated, with a small number of employees and relatively low volume of sales. The legal definition of 'small' often varies by country and industry, but is generally under 100 employees in the United States and under 50 employees in the European Union. In comparison, the definition of mid-sized business by the number of employees is generally under 500 in the U.S. and 250 for the European Union.
   a. Critical Success Factor
   b. Pre-determined overhead rate
   c. Small Business
   d. Golden Boot Compensation

9. _____ is one of the managerial functions like planning, organizing, staffing and directing. It is an important function because it helps to check the errors and to take the corrective action so that deviation from standards are minimized and stated goals of the organization are achieved in desired manner. According to modern concepts, _____ is a foreseeing action whereas earlier concept of _____ was used only when errors were detected. _____ in management means setting standards, measuring actual performance and taking corrective action.
   a. Schedule of reinforcement
   b. Turnover
   c. Decision tree pruning
   d. Control

10. Franchising refers to the methods of practicing and using another person's business philosophy. The _____ grants the independent operator the right to distribute its products, techniques, and trademarks for a percentage of gross monthly sales and a royalty fee. Various tangibles and intangibles such as national or international advertising, training, and other support services are commonly made available by the _____.
    a. 28-hour day
    b. 1990 Clean Air Act
    c. ServiceMaster
    d. Franchisor

11. An _____ is an organization founded and funded by businesses that operate in a specific industry. An industry trade association participates in public relations activities such as advertising, education, political donations, lobbying and publishing, but its main focus is collaboration between companies, or standardization. Associations may offer other services, such as producing conferences, networking or charitable events or offering classes or educational materials.
    a. Industry trade group
    b. A4e
    c. AAAI
    d. A Stake in the Outcome

Chapter 3. Franchising: The Hybrid

12. An _____ is a person who has possession of an enterprise and assumes significant accountability for the inherent risks and the outcome. It is an ambitious leader who combines land, labor, and capital to create and market new goods or services. The term is a loanword from French and was first defined by the Irish economist Richard Cantillon.

   a. Entrepreneur
   b. AAAI
   c. A Stake in the Outcome
   d. A4e

13. _____ is an advertisement in which a particular product specifically mentions a competitor by name for the express purpose of showing why the competitor is inferior to the product naming it.

This should not be confused with parody advertisements, where a fictional product is being advertised for the purpose of poking fun at the particular advertisement, nor should it be confused with the use of a coined brand name for the purpose of comparing the product without actually naming an actual competitor. ('Wikipedia tastes better and is less filling than the Encyclopedia Galactica.')

In the 1980s, during what has been referred to as the cola wars, soft-drink manufacturer Pepsi ran a series of advertisements where people, caught on hidden camera, in a blind taste test, chose Pepsi over rival Coca-Cola.

   a. 33 Strategies of War
   b. 28-hour day
   c. 1990 Clean Air Act
   d. Comparative advertising

14. An _____ is a practitioner of accountancy, which is the measurement, disclosure or provision of assurance about financial information that helps managers, investors, tax authorities and other decision makers make resource allocation decisions.

The word '_____' is derived from the French 'Compter' which took its origin from the Latin 'Computare'. The word was formerly written in English as 'Accomptant', but in process of time the word, which was always pronounced by dropping the 'p', became gradually changed both in pronunciation and in orthography to its present form.

   a. A4e
   b. AAAI
   c. A Stake in the Outcome
   d. Accountant

Chapter 3. Franchising: The Hybrid

15. A _____ is a formal statement of a set of business goals, the reasons why they are believed attainable, and the plan for reaching those goals. It may also contain background information about the organization or team attempting to reach those goals.

The business goals may be defined for for-profit or for non-profit organizations.

 a. Time management
 b. Distributed management
 c. Crisis management
 d. Business plan

16. The term '_____' refers to the concept of collecting information and attempting to spot a pattern in the information. In some fields of study, the term '_____' has more formally-defined meanings.

In project management _____ is a mathematical technique that uses historical results to predict future outcome.

 a. Least squares
 b. Regression analysis
 c. Stepwise regression
 d. Trend analysis

17. _____ is an abbreviation for '_____', a legal document used in the franchising process in the United States.

Franchisors must give a _____ to franchisees at least 10 business days before any contract is signed and before any money changes hands. It contains extensive information about a franchisor, which is intended to give potential franchisees enough information to make educated decisions about their investments.

 a. AAAI
 b. Uniform Franchise Offering Circular
 c. A Stake in the Outcome
 d. A4e

Chapter 4. Successful Business Plans: The Roadmap

1. A _____ is a formal statement of a set of business goals, the reasons why they are believed attainable, and the plan for reaching those goals. It may also contain background information about the organization or team attempting to reach those goals.

   The business goals may be defined for for-profit or for non-profit organizations.

   a. Crisis management
   b. Time management
   c. Distributed management
   d. Business plan

2. An _____ is a person who has possession of an enterprise and assumes significant accountability for the inherent risks and the outcome. It is an ambitious leader who combines land, labor, and capital to create and market new goods or services. The term is a loanword from French and was first defined by the Irish economist Richard Cantillon.
   a. A Stake in the Outcome
   b. A4e
   c. AAAI
   d. Entrepreneur

3. A _____ is a documented investigation of a Market that is used to inform a firm's planning activities particularly around decision of: inventory, purchase, work force expansion/contraction, facility expansion, purchases of capital equipment, promotional activities, and many other aspects of a company.

   Not all managers are asked to conduct a _____, but all managers must make decisions using _____ data and understand how the data was derived. So all managers need a reasonable understanding of the tools most used for making sales forecasts and analyzing markets.

   a. Marketing research
   b. 1990 Clean Air Act
   c. Marketing research process
   d. Market analysis

4. _____ is an integrated communications-based process through which individuals and communities discover that existing and newly-identified needs and wants may be satisfied by the products and services of others.

   _____ is defined by the American _____ Association as the activity, set of institutions, and processes for creating, communicating, delivering, and exchanging offerings that have value for customers, clients, partners, and society at large. The term developed from the original meaning which referred literally to going to market, as in shopping, or going to a market to buy or sell goods or services.

a. Marketing
b. Market development
c. Customer relationship management
d. Disruptive technology

5. _____ is a type of private equity capital typically provided to early-stage, high-potential, growth companies in the interest of generating a return through an eventual realization event such as an IPO or trade sale of the company. _____ investments are generally made as cash in exchange for shares in the invested company. It is typical for _____ investors to identify and back companies in high technology industries such as biotechnology and ICT.

a. Seed round
b. Limited liability corporation
c. Private equity
d. Venture capital

6. An _____ is any party that makes an investment.

The term has taken on a specific meaning in finance to describe the particular types of people and companies that regularly purchase equity or debt securities for financial gain in exchange for funding an expanding company. Less frequently, the term is applied to parties who purchase real estate, currency, commodity derivatives, personal property, or other assets.

a. A Stake in the Outcome
b. Investor
c. AAAI
d. A4e

7. An _____ is a practitioner of accountancy, which is the measurement, disclosure or provision of assurance about financial information that helps managers, investors, tax authorities and other decision makers make resource allocation decisions.

The word '_____' is derived from the French 'Compter' which took its origin from the Latin 'Computare'. The word was formerly written in English as 'Accomptant', but in process of time the word, which was always pronounced by dropping the 'p', became gradually changed both in pronunciation and in orthography to its present form.

a. AAAI
b. A4e
c. A Stake in the Outcome
d. Accountant

8. _____ refers to an assessment of the viability, stability and profitability of a business, sub-business or project.

It is performed by professionals who prepare reports using ratios that make use of information taken from financial statements and other reports. These reports are usually presented to top management as one of their bases in making business decisions.

a. 28-hour day
b. 33 Strategies of War
c. Financial analysis
d. 1990 Clean Air Act

9. In decision theory and estimation theory, the _____ of an estimator, $\hat{\theta}$, of an unknown parameter of the distribution, θ, is the expected value of the loss function

$$R(\theta, \hat{\theta}) = \mathbb{E}_\theta L(\theta, \hat{\theta}) = \int L(\theta, \hat{\theta})\, dP_\theta.$$

where dP_θ is a probability measure parametrized by θ.

- For a scalar parameter θ and a quadratic loss function,

$$L(\theta, \hat{\theta}) = (\theta - \hat{\theta})^2$$

the _____ function becomes the mean squared error of the estimate,

$$R(\theta, \hat{\theta}) = E_\theta(\theta - \hat{\theta})^2$$

- In density estimation, the unknown parameter is probability density itself. The loss function is typically chosen to be a norm in an appropriate function space. For example, for L^2 norm,

$$L(f, \hat{f}) = \|f - \hat{f}\|_2^2$$

the _____ function becomes the mean integrated squared error

$$R(f, \hat{f}) = E\|f - \hat{f}\|^2$$

a. Risk aversion
b. Linear model
c. Financial modeling
d. Risk

Chapter 5. Legal Forms of Ventures: The Structure

1. A _____ also known as a sole trader, or simply proprietorship is a type of business entity which there is only one owner and he has the final word taking all desicions by himself. All debts of the business are debts of the owner and must pay from his personal possessions. This means that the owner has unlimited liabilty.
   a. Golden hello
   b. Foreign ownership
   c. Business rule
   d. Sole proprietorship

2. _____ is the self-government of a nation, country or some portion thereof, generally exercising sovereignty.

   The term _____ is used in contrast to subjugation, which refers to a region as a 'territory' --subject to the political and military control of an external government. The word is sometimes used in a weaker sense to contrast with hegemony, the indirect control of one nation by another, more powerful nation.

   a. AAAI
   b. A Stake in the Outcome
   c. A4e
   d. Independence

3. An _____, for United States federal income tax purposes, is a corporation that makes a valid election to be taxed under Subchapter S of Chapter 1 of the Internal Revenue Code.

   In general, _____s do not pay any income taxes. Instead, the corporation's income or losses are divided among and passed through to its shareholders.

   a. S corporation
   b. 33 Strategies of War
   c. 1990 Clean Air Act
   d. 28-hour day

4. _____ according to Onuoha (2007) is the practice of starting new organizations or revitalizing mature organizations, particularly new businesses generally in response to identified opportunities. _____ is often a difficult undertaking, as a vast majority of new businesses fail. Entrepreneurial activities are substantially different depending on the type of organization that is being started.
   a. A Stake in the Outcome
   b. Entrepreneurship
   c. AAAI
   d. A4e

Chapter 5. Legal Forms of Ventures: The Structure 21

5. A _____ is a type of business entity in which partners (owners) share with each other the profits or losses of the business. _____s are often favored over corporations for taxation purposes, as the _____ structure does not generally incur a tax on profits before it is distributed to the partners (i.e. there is no dividend tax levied.) However, depending on the _____ structure and the jurisdiction in which it operates, owners of a _____ may be exposed to greater personal liability than they would as shareholders of a corporation.
   a. Federal Employers Liability Act
   b. Due process
   c. Mediation
   d. Partnership

6. In the commercial and legal parlance of most countries, a _____ or simply a partnership, refers to an association of persons or an unincorporated company with the following major features:

   - Created by agreement, proof of existence and estoppel.
   - Formed by two or more persons
   - The owners are all personally liable for any legal actions and debts the company may face

   It is a partnership in which partners share equally in both responsibility and liability.

   Partnerships have certain default characteristics relating to both the relationship between the individual partners and (b) the relationship between the partnership and the outside world. The former can generally be overridden by agreement between the partners, whereas the latter generally cannot be.

   The assets of the business are owned on behalf of the other partners, and they are each personally liable, jointly and severally, for business debts, taxes or tortious liability.

   a. Prospero Business Suite
   b. Business Roundtable
   c. National Center for Trauma-Informed Care
   d. General partnership

7. A _____ is a form of partnership similar to a general partnership, except that in addition to one or more general partners (GPs), there are one or more limited partners (_____s.) It is a partnership in which only one partner is required to be a general partner.

   The GPs are, in all major respects, in the same legal position as partners in a conventional firm, i.e. they have management control, share the right to use partnership property, share the profits of the firm in predefined proportions, and have joint and several liability for the debts of the partnership.

Chapter 5. Legal Forms of Ventures: The Structure

a. Private equity
b. Growth capital
c. Pension fund
d. Limited Partnership

8. A limited partnership is a form of partnership similar to a general partnership, except that in addition to one or more general partners (GPs), there are one or more _____ It is a partnership in which only one partner is required to be a general partner.

The GPs are, in all major respects, in the same legal position as partners in a conventional firm, i.e. they have management control, share the right to use partnership property, share the profits of the firm in predefined proportions, and have joint and several liability for the debts of the partnership.

a. Growth capital
b. Venture Capitalist
c. Limited partnership
d. Limited partners

9. The _____, which includes its 1976 revision called the Revised _____, is a uniform act (similar to a model statute), proposed by the National Conference of Commissioners on Uniform State Laws ('NCCUSL') for the governance of business partnerships by U.S. States. The NCCUSL promulgated the original _____ in 1916 and the most recent revision in 2001.

The NCCUSL promulgated the original _____ in 1916, which is now called the _____ (1916) or _____ (1916); a 1976 revision named the Revised _____ which is also now called the _____ (1976), _____ (1976) or RUniform Limited Partnership Act (1976); a 1985 revision named _____ (1976) with 1985 Amendments, which is also now called _____ (1985) or RUniform Limited Partnership Act (1985); and a 2001 revision that was colloquially called Re-RUniform Limited Partnership Act during the drafting process but then was officially named the _____ (2001) or _____ (2001.)

a. AAAI
b. A4e
c. A Stake in the Outcome
d. Uniform Limited Partnership Act

10. An _____ is a person who has possession of an enterprise and assumes significant accountability for the inherent risks and the outcome. It is an ambitious leader who combines land, labor, and capital to create and market new goods or services. The term is a loanword from French and was first defined by the Irish economist Richard Cantillon.

a. A Stake in the Outcome
b. Entrepreneur
c. A4e
d. AAAI

11. _____ is a concept whereby a person's financial liability is limited to a fixed sum, most commonly the value of a person's investment in a company or partnership with _____. In other words, if a company with _____ is sued, then the plaintiffs are suing the company, not its owners or investors. A shareholder in a limited company is not personally liable for any of the debts of the company, other than for the value of his investment in that company.
   a. Partnership
   b. Toxic Substances Control Act
   c. Limited liability
   d. Privity

12. In the United Kingdom _____s are governed by the _____s Act 2000 (in England and Wales and Scotland) and the _____s Act (Northern Ireland) 2002 in Northern Ireland. A UK _____ is a Corporate body - that is to say, it has a continuing legal existence independent of its Members, as compared to a Partnership which may (in England and Wales they do not) have a legal existence dependent upon its Membership.

A UK _____'s members have a collective ('Joint') responsibility, to the extent that they may agree in an '_____ agreement', but no individual ('several') responsibility for each other's actions.

   a. Limited liability partnership
   b. Small and medium enterprises
   c. Chief risk officer
   d. Compensation methods

13. A _____ in the law of the vast majority of United States jurisdictions is a legal form of business company that provides limited liability to its owners. Often incorrectly called a 'limited liability corporation' (instead of company), it is a hybrid business entity having certain characteristics of both a corporation and a partnership or sole proprietorship (depending on how many owners there are.) The primary characteristic an _____ shares with a corporation is limited liability, and the primary characteristic it shares with a partnership is the availability of pass-through income taxation.
   a. Growth capital
   b. Limited partners
   c. Limited liability company
   d. Venture Capitalist

14. In finance, an _____ is a contract between a buyer and a seller that gives the buyer the right--but not the obligation-- to buy or to sell a particular asset (the underlying asset) at a later day at an agreed price. In return for granting the _____, the seller collects a payment (the premium) from the buyer. A call _____ gives the buyer the right to buy the underlying asset; a put _____ gives the buyer of the _____ the right to sell the underlying asset.
   a. A4e
   b. A Stake in the Outcome
   c. AAAI
   d. Option

Chapter 6. Market Research: The Niche

1. A _____ is a documented investigation of a Market that is used to inform a firm's planning activities particularly around decision of: inventory, purchase, work force expansion/contraction, facility expansion, purchases of capital equipment, promotional activities, and many other aspects of a company.

Not all managers are asked to conduct a _____, but all managers must make decisions using _____ data and understand how the data was derived. So all managers need a reasonable understanding of the tools most used for making sales forecasts and analyzing markets.

   a. 1990 Clean Air Act
   b. Marketing research
   c. Market analysis
   d. Marketing research process

2. A niche market is the subset of the market on which a specific product is focusing on; Therefore the _____ defines the specific product features aimed at satisfying specific market needs, as well as the price range, production quality and the demographics that is intended to impact.

Every single product that is on sale can be defined by its niche market. As of special note, the products aimed at a wide demographics audience, with the resulting low price (due to Price elasticity of demand), are said to belong to the Mainstream niche, in practice referred only as Mainstream or of high demand.

   a. Prevailing wage
   b. Market niche
   c. Labor intensive
   d. Dominant logic

3. In economics, business, retail, and accounting, a _____ is the value of money that has been used up to produce something, and hence is not available for use anymore. In economics, a _____ is an alternative that is given up as a result of a decision. In business, the _____ may be one of acquisition, in which case the amount of money expended to acquire it is counted as _____.
   a. Fixed costs
   b. Cost allocation
   c. Cost
   d. Cost overrun

4. _____ is a concept developed by Michael Porter, used in business strategy. It describes a way to establish the competitive advantage. _____, in basic words, means the lowest cost of operation in the industry.

a. Cost leadership
b. Strategic business unit
c. Switching cost
d. Strategic group

5. In economics, a _____ exists when a specific individual or enterprise has sufficient control over a particular product or service to determine significantly the terms on which other individuals shall have access to it. Monopolies are thus characterized by a lack of economic competition for the good or service that they provide and a lack of viable substitute goods. The verb 'monopolize' refers to the process by which a firm gains persistently greater market share than what is expected under perfect competition.

a. 1990 Clean Air Act
b. 28-hour day
c. 33 Strategies of War
d. Monopoly

6. An _____ is a market form in which a market or industry is dominated by a small number of sellers (oligopolists.) Because there are few participants in this type of market, each oligopolist is aware of the actions of the others. The decisions of one firm influence, and are influenced by, the decisions of other firms.

a. A Stake in the Outcome
b. A4e
c. AAAI
d. Oligopoly

7. _____ has been described as the 'process of social influence in which one person can enlist the aid and support of others in the accomplishment of a common task'. A definition more inclusive of followers comes from Alan Keith of Genentech who said '_____ is ultimately about creating a way for people to contribute to making something extraordinary happen.'

_____ is one of the most salient aspects of the organizational context. However, defining _____ has been challenging.

a. 28-hour day
b. 1990 Clean Air Act
c. Leadership
d. Situational leadership

8. _____ of the learning curve effect and the closely related experience curve effect express the relationship between equations for experience and efficiency or between efficiency gains and investment in the effort. The experience of 'learning curves' was first observed by the 19th Century German psychologist Hermann Ebbinghaus according to the difficulty of memorizing varying numbers of verbal stimuli, and subsequent learning about the complex processes of learning are discussed in the

.

The rule used for representing the learning curve effect states that the more times a task has been performed, the less time will be required on each subsequent iteration.

a. Distribution
b. Spatial Decision Support Systems
c. Point biserial correlation coefficient
d. Models

9. The term '_____' refers to the concept of collecting information and attempting to spot a pattern in the information. In some fields of study, the term '_____' has more formally-defined meanings.

In project management _____ is a mathematical technique that uses historical results to predict future outcome.

a. Least squares
b. Trend analysis
c. Stepwise regression
d. Regression analysis

10. _____ is a broad label that refers to any individuals or households that use goods and services generated within the economy. The concept of a _____ is used in different contexts, so that the usage and significance of the term may vary.

Typically when business people and economists talk of _____s they are talking about person as _____, an aggregated commodity item with little individuality other than that expressed in the buy/not-buy decision.

a. Consumer
b. 28-hour day
c. 1990 Clean Air Act
d. 33 Strategies of War

Chapter 6. Market Research: The Niche

11. _____ is an integrated communications-based process through which individuals and communities discover that existing and newly-identified needs and wants may be satisfied by the products and services of others.

_____ is defined by the American _____ Association as the activity, set of institutions, and processes for creating, communicating, delivering, and exchanging offerings that have value for customers, clients, partners, and society at large. The term developed from the original meaning which referred literally to going to market, as in shopping, or going to a market to buy or sell goods or services.

   a. Market development
   b. Disruptive technology
   c. Customer relationship management
   d. Marketing

12. Consumer market research is a form of applied sociology that concentrates on understanding the behaviours, whims and preferences, of consumers in a market-based economy, and aims to understand the effects and comparative success of marketing campaigns. The field of consumer _____ as a statistical science was pioneered by Arthur Nielsen with the founding of the ACNielsen Company in 1923.

Thus _____ is the systematic and objective identification, collection, analysis, and dissemination of information for the purpose of assisting management in decision making related to the identification and solution of problems and opportunities in marketing.

   a. Marketing research
   b. Market analysis
   c. Marketing research process
   d. 1990 Clean Air Act

13. A _____ is a business that is privately owned and operated, with a small number of employees and relatively low volume of sales. The legal definition of 'small' often varies by country and industry, but is generally under 100 employees in the United States and under 50 employees in the European Union. In comparison, the definition of mid-sized business by the number of employees is generally under 500 in the U.S. and 250 for the European Union.
   a. Pre-determined overhead rate
   b. Critical Success Factor
   c. Golden Boot Compensation
   d. Small business

14. In economics, _____ is the desire to own something and the ability to pay for it. The term _____ signifies the ability or the willingness to buy a particular commodity at a given point of time.

a. 28-hour day
b. 33 Strategies of War
c. Demand
d. 1990 Clean Air Act

15. _____ is a mathematical science pertaining to the collection, analysis, interpretation or explanation, and presentation of data. It also provides tools for prediction and forecasting based on data. It is applicable to a wide variety of academic disciplines, from the natural and social sciences to the humanities, government and business.

a. Simple moving average
b. Statistics
c. Location parameter
d. Failure rate

16. _____ is a business magazine published by McGraw-Hill. It was first published in 1929 (as The Business Week) under the direction of Malcolm Muir, who was serving as president of the McGraw-Hill Publishing company at the time. Its primary competitors in the national business magazine category are Fortune and Forbes, which are published bi-weekly.

a. Democracy in America
b. Hotel Vikas
c. The Wealth of Nations
d. BusinessWeek

17. A _____ is a form of qualitative research in which a group of people are asked about their attitude towards a product, service, concept, advertisement, idea, or packaging. Questions are asked in an interactive group setting where participants are free to talk with other group members.

The first _____s were created at the Bureau of Applied Social Research by associate director, sociologist Robert K. Merton.

a. 1990 Clean Air Act
b. Marketing research
c. Market analysis
d. Focus group

18. A _____ is a research instrument consisting of a series of questions and other prompts for the purpose of gathering information from respondents. Although they are often designed for statistical analysis of the responses, this is not always the case. The _____ was invented by Sir Francis Galton.

a. Questionnaire
b. Structured interview
c. Questionnaire construction
d. Mystery shoppers

19. _____ is a contract between two parties, one being the employer and the other being the employee. An employee may be defined as: 'A person in the service of another under any contract of hire, express or implied, oral or written, where the employer has the power or right to control and direct the employee in the material details of how the work is to be performed.' Black's Law Dictionary page 471 (5th ed. 1979.)
a. Employment rate
b. Exit interview
c. Employment counsellor
d. Employment

20. _____ systems are rule-based systems that are able to automatically provide solutions to repetitive management problems (Turban, Leidner, McLean and Wetherbe, 2007.) _____s are very closely related to business informatics and business analytics.

_____ systems are based on business rules.

a. Automated decision support
b. Entertainment Management
c. Executive development
d. Efficient Consumer Response

21. _____ generally refers to a list of all planned expenses and revenues. It is a plan for saving and spending. A _____ is an important concept in microeconomics, which uses a _____ line to illustrate the trade-offs between two or more goods.
a. 28-hour day
b. 33 Strategies of War
c. 1990 Clean Air Act
d. Budget

22. A _____ is a formal statement of a set of business goals, the reasons why they are believed attainable, and the plan for reaching those goals. It may also contain background information about the organization or team attempting to reach those goals.

The business goals may be defined for for-profit or for non-profit organizations.

a. Business plan
b. Distributed management
c. Time management
d. Crisis management

Chapter 7. Strategic Pricing: The Hook

1. _____ is one of the four Ps of the marketing mix. The other three aspects are product, promotion, and place. It is also a key variable in microeconomic price allocation theory.
   a. Transfer pricing
   b. Penetration pricing
   c. Price floor
   d. Pricing

2. _____ is an advertisement in which a particular product specifically mentions a competitor by name for the express purpose of showing why the competitor is inferior to the product naming it.

This should not be confused with parody advertisements, where a fictional product is being advertised for the purpose of poking fun at the particular advertisement, nor should it be confused with the use of a coined brand name for the purpose of comparing the product without actually naming an actual competitor. ('Wikipedia tastes better and is less filling than the Encyclopedia Galactica.')

In the 1980s, during what has been referred to as the cola wars, soft-drink manufacturer Pepsi ran a series of advertisements where people, caught on hidden camera, in a blind taste test, chose Pepsi over rival Coca-Cola.

   a. Comparative advertising
   b. 1990 Clean Air Act
   c. 33 Strategies of War
   d. 28-hour day

3. _____ is an integrated communications-based process through which individuals and communities discover that existing and newly-identified needs and wants may be satisfied by the products and services of others.

   _____ is defined by the American _____ Association as the activity, set of institutions, and processes for creating, communicating, delivering, and exchanging offerings that have value for customers, clients, partners, and society at large. The term developed from the original meaning which referred literally to going to market, as in shopping, or going to a market to buy or sell goods or services.

   a. Market development
   b. Disruptive technology
   c. Customer relationship management
   d. Marketing

4. A _____ is a process that can allow an organization to concentrate its limited resources on the greatest opportunities to increase sales and achieve a sustainable competitive advantage. A _____ should be centered around the key concept that customer satisfaction is the main goal.

Chapter 7. Strategic Pricing: The Hook

A _____ is a written plan which combines product development, promotion, distribution, and pricing approach, identifies the firm's marketing goals, and explains how they will be achieved within a stated timeframe.

   a. Category management
   b. Disruptive technology
   c. Product bundling
   d. Marketing strategy

5. In economics, business, retail, and accounting, a _____ is the value of money that has been used up to produce something, and hence is not available for use anymore. In economics, a _____ is an alternative that is given up as a result of a decision. In business, the _____ may be one of acquisition, in which case the amount of money expended to acquire it is counted as _____.
   a. Cost allocation
   b. Cost overrun
   c. Cost
   d. Fixed costs

6. In economics, _____ is the desire to own something and the ability to pay for it. The term _____ signifies the ability or the willingness to buy a particular commodity at a given point of time.
   a. 1990 Clean Air Act
   b. 33 Strategies of War
   c. 28-hour day
   d. Demand

7. _____ is the pricing technique of setting a relatively low initial entry price, often lower than the eventual market price, to attract new customers. The strategy works on the expectation that customers will switch to the new brand because of the lower price. _____ is most commonly associated with a marketing objective of increasing market share or sales volume, rather than to make profit in the short term.
   a. Pricing objectives
   b. Transfer pricing
   c. Price war
   d. Penetration pricing

8. _____ or price ending is a marketing practice based on the theory that certain prices have a psychological impact. The retail prices are often expressed as 'odd prices': a little less than a round number, e.g. $19.99 or £6.95 (but not necessarily mathematically odd, it could also be 2.98.) The theory is this drives demand greater than would be expected if consumers were perfectly rational.

a. Business rule
b. Golden hello
c. Planning horizon
d. Psychological pricing

9. A niche market is the subset of the market on which a specific product is focusing on; Therefore the _____ defines the specific product features aimed at satisfying specific market needs, as well as the price range, production quality and the demographics that is intended to impact.

Every single product that is on sale can be defined by its niche market. As of special note, the products aimed at a wide demographics audience, with the resulting low price (due to Price elasticity of demand), are said to belong to the Mainstream niche, in practice referred only as Mainstream or of high demand.

a. Labor intensive
b. Dominant logic
c. Prevailing wage
d. Market niche

10. Wholesaling, jobbing to industrial, commercial, institutional or to other _____ and related subordinated services.

According to the United Nations Statistics Division, 'wholesale' is the resale (sale without transformation) of new and used goods to retailers, to industrial, commercial, institutional or professional users or involves acting as an agent or broker in buying merchandise for such persons or companies. _____ frequently physically assemble, sort and grade goods in large lots, break bulk, repack and redistribute in smaller lots.

a. Supply chain
b. Wholesalers
c. Supply chain management
d. Packaging

11. _____, Gross profit margin or Gross Profit Rate can be defined as the amount of contribution to the business enterprise, after paying for direct-fixed and direct-variable unit costs, required to cover overheads (fixed commitments) and provide a buffer for unknown items. It expresses the relationship between gross profit and sales revenue.

It can be expressed in absolute terms:

Gross Profit = Revenue − Cost of Sales

or as the ratio of gross profit to sales revenue, usually in the form of a percentage:

_____ Percentage = (Revenue-Cost of Sales)/Revenue

Cost of Sales includes variable costs and fixed costs directly linked to the product, such as material and labor.

a. Gross margin
b. 1990 Clean Air Act
c. Profit maximization
d. Profit margin

12. _____ is the difference between the cost of a good or service and its selling price. A _____ is added on to the total cost incurred by the producer of a good or service in order to create a profit. The total cost reflects the total amount of both fixed and variable expenses to produce and distribute a product.
a. Premium pricing
b. Price points
c. Topics
d. Markup

13. _____ Management is the succession of strategies used by management as a product goes through its _____. The conditions in which a product is sold changes over time and must be managed as it moves through its succession of stages.

The _____ goes through many phases, involves many professional disciplines, and requires many skills, tools and processes.

a. Job hunting
b. Golden handshake
c. Strategic Alliance
d. Product life cycle

14. Price _____ is defined as the measure of responsiveness in the quantity demanded for a commodity as a result of change in price of the same commodity. It is a measure of how consumers react to a change in price. In other words, it is percentage change in quantity demanded by the percentage change in price of the same commodity.
a. A4e
b. AAAI
c. A Stake in the Outcome
d. Elasticity of demand

15. _____ is a business management strategy aimed at embedding awareness of quality in all organizational processes. _____ has been widely used in manufacturing, education, hospitals, call centers, government, and service industries, as well as NASA space and science programs.

As defined by the International Organization for Standardization (ISO):

'_____ is a management approach for an organization, centered on quality, based on the participation of all its members and aiming at long-term success through customer satisfaction, and benefits to all members of the organization and to society.' ISO 8402:1994

One major aim is to reduce variation from every process so that greater consistency of effort is obtained. (Royse, D., Thyer, B., Padgett D., ' Logan T., 2006)

a. 1990 Clean Air Act
b. Total quality management
c. 28-hour day
d. Quality management

16. _____ can be considered to have three main components: quality control, quality assurance and quality improvement. _____ is focused not only on product quality, but also the means to achieve it. _____ therefore uses quality assurance and control of processes as well as products to achieve more consistent quality.

a. 1990 Clean Air Act
b. Total quality management
c. 28-hour day
d. Quality management

17. _____ consists of the sale of goods or merchandise from a fixed location, such as a department store, boutique or kiosk in small or individual lots for direct consumption by the purchaser. _____ may include subordinated services, such as delivery. Purchasers may be individuals or businesses.

a. 28-hour day
b. Planogram
c. 1990 Clean Air Act
d. Retailing

18. _____ is the strategic and coherent approach to the management of an organisation's most valued assets - the people working there who individually and collectively contribute to the achievement of the objectives of the business. The terms '_____' and 'human resources' (HR) have largely replaced the term 'personnel management' as a description of the processes involved in managing people in organizations. In simple sense, _____ means employing people, developing their resources, utilizing, maintaining and compensating their services in tune with the job and organizational requirement.

a. Revolving door syndrome
b. Progressive discipline
c. Job knowledge
d. Human resource management

19. _____ is a process of agreeing upon objectives within an organization so that management and employees agree to the objectives and understand what they are in the organization.

The term '_____' was first popularized by Peter Drucker in his 1954 book 'The Practice of Management'.

The essence of _____ is participative goal setting, choosing course of actions and decision making.

a. Management by objectives
b. Job enrichment
c. Clean sheet review
d. Business economics

Chapter 8. Start-Up Capital: The Injection

1. In business and accounting, _____s are everything of value that is owned by a person or company. Any property or object of value that one possesses, usually considered as applicable to the payment of one's debts is considered an _____. Simplistically stated, _____s are things of value that can be readily converted into cash.
   a. A Stake in the Outcome
   b. A4e
   c. AAAI
   d. Asset

2. In financial accounting, a _____ or statement of financial position is a summary of a person's or organization's balances. Assets, liabilities and ownership equity are listed as of a specific date, such as the end of its financial year. A _____ is often described as a snapshot of a company's financial condition.
   a. 1990 Clean Air Act
   b. 33 Strategies of War
   c. Balance sheet
   d. 28-hour day

3. _____ refers to the movement of cash into or out of a business or financial product. It is usually measured during a specified, finite period of time. Measurement of _____ can be used

   - to determine a project's rate of return or value. The time of _____s into and out of projects are used as inputs in financial models such as internal rate of return, and net present value.
   - to determine problems with a business's liquidity. Being profitable does not necessarily mean being liquid. A company can fail because of a shortage of cash, even while profitable.
   - as an alternate measure of a business's profits when it is believed that accrual accounting concepts do not represent economic realities. For example, a company may be notionally profitable but generating little operational cash (as may be the case for a company that barters its products rather than selling for cash.) In such a case, the company may be deriving additional operating cash by issuing shares evaluating default risk, re-investment requirements, etc.

   _____ is a generic term used differently depending on the context. It may be defined by users for their own purposes.

   a. Sweat equity
   b. Cash flow
   c. Gross profit
   d. Gross profit margin

4. In economics, business, retail, and accounting, a _____ is the value of money that has been used up to produce something, and hence is not available for use anymore. In economics, a _____ is an alternative that is given up as a result of a decision. In business, the _____ may be one of acquisition, in which case the amount of money expended to acquire it is counted as _____.

a. Fixed costs
b. Cost overrun
c. Cost
d. Cost allocation

5. In financial accounting, _____ or cost of sales includes the direct costs attributable to the production of the goods sold by a company. This amount includes the materials cost used in creating the goods along with the direct labour costs used to produce the good. It excludes indirect expenses such as distribution costs and sales force costs.

a. 1990 Clean Air Act
b. Reorder point
c. 28-hour day
d. Cost of goods sold

6. In accounting, a _____ is an asset on the balance sheet which is expected to be sold or otherwise used up in the near future, usually within one year, or one business cycle - whichever is longer. Typical _____s include cash, cash equivalents, accounts receivable, inventory, the portion of prepaid accounts which will be used within a year, and short-term investments.

On the balance sheet, assets will typically be classified into _____s and long-term assets.

a. Net income
b. Treasury stock
c. Matching principle
d. Current asset

7. In finance, _____ are considered liabilities of the business that are to be settled in cash within the fiscal year or the operating cycle, whichever period is longer.

For example accounts payable for goods, services or supplies that were purchased for use in the operation of the business and payable within a normal period of time would be _____.

Bonds, mortgages and loans that are payable over a term exceeding one year would be fixed liabilities.

a. Depreciation
b. Matching principle
c. Current liabilities
d. Generally accepted accounting principles

8. _____ is a term used in accounting, economics and finance to spread the cost of an asset over the span of several years.

In simple words we can say that _____ is the reduction in the value of an asset due to usage, passage of time, wear and tear, technological outdating or obsolescence, depletion, inadequacy, rot, rust, decay or other such factors.

In accounting, _____ is a term used to describe any method of attributing the historical or purchase cost of an asset across its useful life, roughly corresponding to normal wear and tear.

   a. Matching principle
   b. Net profit
   c. Treasury stock
   d. Depreciation

9. _____ are formal records of the financial activities of a business, person, or other entity. In British English, including United Kingdom company law, _____ are often referred to as accounts, although the term _____ is also used, particularly by accountants.

_____ provide an overview of a business or person's financial condition in both short and long term.

   a. 28-hour day
   b. 1990 Clean Air Act
   c. Financial statements
   d. 33 Strategies of War

10. In accounting, _____ or sales profit is the difference between revenue and the cost of making a product or providing a service, before deducting overhead, payroll, taxation, and interest payments. Note that this is different from operating profit (earnings before interest and taxes.)

Net sales are calculated:

   Net sales = Sales - Sales returns and allowances.

   a. Cash flow
   b. Gross profit margin
   c. Capital budgeting
   d. Gross profit

Chapter 8. Start-Up Capital: The Injection

11. _____ is a company's financial statement that indicates how the revenue is transformed into the net income The purpose of the _____ is to show managers and investors whether the company made or lost money during the period being reported.

The important thing to remember about an _____ is that it represents a period of time.

a. A4e
b. A Stake in the Outcome
c. AAAI
d. Income statement

12. An _____ is a person who has possession of an enterprise and assumes significant accountability for the inherent risks and the outcome. It is an ambitious leader who combines land, labor, and capital to create and market new goods or services. The term is a loanword from French and was first defined by the Irish economist Richard Cantillon.

a. Entrepreneur
b. AAAI
c. A Stake in the Outcome
d. A4e

13. _____ is the capital that a business raises by taking out a loan. It is a loan made to a company that is normally repaid at some future date. _____ differs from equity or share capital because subscribers to _____ do not become part owners of the business, but are merely creditors, and the suppliers of _____ usually receive a contractually fixed annual percentage return on their loan, and this is known as the coupon rate.

a. Novated lease
b. Net worth
c. Market value added
d. Debt capital

14. In business and finance accounting, _____ is equal to the gross profit minus overheads minus interest payable plus/minus one off items for a given time period (usually: accounting period.)

A common synonym for '_____' when discussing financial statements (which include a balance sheet and an income statement) is the bottom line. This term results from the traditional appearance of an income statement which shows all allocated revenues and expenses over a specified time period with the resulting summation on the bottom line of the report.

Chapter 8. Start-Up Capital: The Injection

   a. Net profit
   b. Matching principle
   c. Generally accepted accounting principles
   d. Treasury stock

15. _____ is a financial metric which represents operating liquidity available to a business. Along with fixed assets such as plant and equipment, _____ is considered a part of operating capital. It is calculated as current assets minus current liabilities.
   a. 1990 Clean Air Act
   b. 28-hour day
   c. 33 Strategies of War
   d. Working capital

16. A _____ is a person or investment firm that makes venture investments, and these _____s are expected to bring managerial and technical expertise as well as capital to their investments. A venture capital fund refers to a pooled investment vehicle that primarily invests the financial capital of third-party investors in enterprises that are too risky for the standard capital markets or bank loans.

Venture capital is also associated with job creation, the knowledge economy and used as a proxy measure of innovation within an economic sector or geography.

   a. Limited liability corporation
   b. Limited partners
   c. Private equity
   d. Venture capitalist

17. _____ is a contract between two parties, one being the employer and the other being the employee. An employee may be defined as: 'A person in the service of another under any contract of hire, express or implied, oral or written, where the employer has the power or right to control and direct the employee in the material details of how the work is to be performed.' Black's Law Dictionary page 471 (5th ed. 1979.)
   a. Exit interview
   b. Employment counsellor
   c. Employment rate
   d. Employment

18. An _____ is any party that makes an investment.

The term has taken on a specific meaning in finance to describe the particular types of people and companies that regularly purchase equity or debt securities for financial gain in exchange for funding an expanding company. Less frequently, the term is applied to parties who purchase real estate, currency, commodity derivatives, personal property, or other assets.

a. AAAI
b. A Stake in the Outcome
c. A4e
d. Investor

19. _____ exists when one firm provides goods or services to a customer with an agreement to bill them later, or receive a shipment or service from a supplier under an agreement to pay them later. It can be viewed as an essential element of capitalization in an operating business because it can reduce the required capital investment to operate the business if it is managed properly. _____ is the largest use of capital for a majority of business to business (B2B) sellers in the United States and is a critical source of capital for a majority of all businesses.

a. Countertrade
b. Trade credit
c. 1990 Clean Air Act
d. Buy-sell agreement

20. A _____ is any credit source extended to a business by a bank or financial institution. A _____ may take several forms such as cash credit, overdraft, demand loan, export packing credit, term loan, discounting or purchase of commercial bills etc. It is like an account that can readily be tapped into if the need arises or not touched at all and saved for emergencies.

a. 28-hour day
b. 1990 Clean Air Act
c. 33 Strategies of War
d. Line of credit

21. _____ is an advertisement in which a particular product specifically mentions a competitor by name for the express purpose of showing why the competitor is inferior to the product naming it.

This should not be confused with parody advertisements, where a fictional product is being advertised for the purpose of poking fun at the particular advertisement, nor should it be confused with the use of a coined brand name for the purpose of comparing the product without actually naming an actual competitor. ('Wikipedia tastes better and is less filling than the Encyclopedia Galactica.')

In the 1980s, during what has been referred to as the cola wars, soft-drink manufacturer Pepsi ran a series of advertisements where people, caught on hidden camera, in a blind taste test, chose Pepsi over rival Coca-Cola.

a. 1990 Clean Air Act
b. 28-hour day
c. Comparative advertising
d. 33 Strategies of War

22. A _____ is a business that is privately owned and operated, with a small number of employees and relatively low volume of sales. The legal definition of 'small' often varies by country and industry, but is generally under 100 employees in the United States and under 50 employees in the European Union. In comparison, the definition of mid-sized business by the number of employees is generally under 500 in the U.S. and 250 for the European Union.
   a. Critical Success Factor
   b. Small business
   c. Golden Boot Compensation
   d. Pre-determined overhead rate

23. A _____ is a relatively new executive level position at a corporation, company, organization typically reporting directly to the CEO or board of directors. The _____ is responsible for a brand's image, experience, and promise, and propagating it throughout all aspects of the company. The brand officer oversees marketing, advertising, design, public relations and customer service departments.
   a. Chief brand officer
   b. Chief executive officer
   c. Director of communications
   d. Purchasing manager

Chapter 9. Financial Statements: The Scorecard

1. In business and accounting, _____s are everything of value that is owned by a person or company. Any property or object of value that one possesses, usually considered as applicable to the payment of one's debts is considered an _____. Simplistically stated, _____s are things of value that can be readily converted into cash.
    a. Asset
    b. AAAI
    c. A Stake in the Outcome
    d. A4e

2. In financial accounting, a _____ or statement of financial position is a summary of a person's or organization's balances. Assets, liabilities and ownership equity are listed as of a specific date, such as the end of its financial year. A _____ is often described as a snapshot of a company's financial condition.
    a. 33 Strategies of War
    b. 28-hour day
    c. 1990 Clean Air Act
    d. Balance sheet

3. _____ are formal records of the financial activities of a business, person, or other entity. In British English, including United Kingdom company law, _____ are often referred to as accounts, although the term _____ is also used, particularly by accountants.

    _____ provide an overview of a business or person's financial condition in both short and long term.

    a. 1990 Clean Air Act
    b. 33 Strategies of War
    c. 28-hour day
    d. Financial statements

4. In accounting, a _____ is an asset on the balance sheet which is expected to be sold or otherwise used up in the near future, usually within one year, or one business cycle - whichever is longer. Typical _____s include cash, cash equivalents, accounts receivable, inventory, the portion of prepaid accounts which will be used within a year, and short-term investments.

    On the balance sheet, assets will typically be classified into _____s and long-term assets.

    a. Net income
    b. Treasury stock
    c. Current asset
    d. Matching principle

Chapter 9. Financial Statements: The Scorecard

5. _____ are defined as identifiable non-monetary assets that cannot be seen, touched or physically measured, which are created through time and/or effort and that are identifiable as a separate asset. There are two primary forms of intangibles - legal intangibles (such as trade secrets (e.g., customer lists), copyrights, patents, trademarks, and goodwill) and competitive intangibles (such as knowledge activities (know-how, knowledge), collaboration activities, leverage activities, and structural activities.) Legal intangibles are known under the generic term intellectual property and generate legal property rights defensible in a court of law.

   a. Interlocking directorate
   b. Induction programme
   c. Employee value proposition
   d. Intangible assets

6. _____ is one of a series of accounting transactions dealing with the billing of customers who owe money to a person, company or organization for goods and services that have been provided to the customer. In most business entities this is typically done by generating an invoice and mailing or electronically delivering it to the customer, who in turn must pay it within an established timeframe called credit or payment terms.

An example of a common payment term is Net 30, meaning payment is due in the amount of the invoice 30 days from the date of invoice.

   a. Accumulated Depreciation
   b. Other revenue
   c. A Stake in the Outcome
   d. Accounts receivable

7. Book Value = Original Cost - _____

Book value at the end of year becomes book value at the beginning of next year. The asset is depreciated until the book value equals scrap value.

If the vehicle were to be sold and the sales price exceeded the depreciated value (net book value) then the excess would be considered a gain and subject to depreciation recapture.

   a. Accumulated depreciation
   b. A Stake in the Outcome
   c. Other revenue
   d. Accounts receivable

8. _____ is a term used in accounting, economics and finance to spread the cost of an asset over the span of several years.

In simple words we can say that _____ is the reduction in the value of an asset due to usage, passage of time, wear and tear, technological outdating or obsolescence, depletion, inadequacy, rot, rust, decay or other such factors.

In accounting, _____ is a term used to describe any method of attributing the historical or purchase cost of an asset across its useful life, roughly corresponding to normal wear and tear.

   a. Depreciation
   b. Matching principle
   c. Treasury stock
   d. Net profit

9. _____ plant, and equipment, is a term used in accountancy for assets and property which cannot easily be converted into cash. This can be compared with current assets such as cash or bank accounts, which are described as liquid assets. In most cases, only tangible assets are referred to as fixed.
   a. 28-hour day
   b. 1990 Clean Air Act
   c. Fixed asset
   d. 33 Strategies of War

10. _____ is a file or account that contains money that a person or company owes to suppliers, but has not paid yet (a form of debt.) When you receive an invoice you add it to the file, and then you remove it when you pay. Thus, the A/P is a form of credit that suppliers offer to their purchasers by allowing them to pay for a product or service after it has already been received.
   a. A Stake in the Outcome
   b. Accounts payable
   c. Accounts receivable
   d. Other revenue

11. _____ is a form of corporate equity ownership, a type of security. It is called 'common' to distinguish it from preferred stock. In the event of bankruptcy, _____ investors receive their funds after preferred stock holders, bondholders, creditors, etc.
   a. Free riding
   b. Stockholder
   c. 1990 Clean Air Act
   d. Common stock

Chapter 9. Financial Statements: The Scorecard

12. _____ is the price at which an asset would trade in a competitive Walrasian auction setting. _____ is often used interchangeably with open _____, fair value or fair _____, although these terms have distinct definitions in different standards, and may differ in some circumstances.

International Valuation Standards defines _____ as 'the estimated amount for which a property should exchange on the date of valuation between a willing buyer and a willing seller in an arm's-length transaction after proper marketing wherein the parties had each acted knowledgeably, prudently, and without compulsion.'

_____ is a concept distinct from market price, which is 'the price at which one can transact', while _____ is 'the true underlying value' according to theoretical standards.

a. Restructuring
b. Payback period
c. Market value added
d. Market value

13. _____ is a company's financial statement that indicates how the revenue is transformed into the net income The purpose of the _____ is to show managers and investors whether the company made or lost money during the period being reported.

The important thing to remember about an _____ is that it represents a period of time.

a. A Stake in the Outcome
b. A4e
c. AAAI
d. Income statement

14. _____ is equal to the income that a firm has after subtracting costs and expenses from the total revenue. _____ can be distributed among holders of common stock as a dividend or held by the firm as retained earnings. _____ is an accounting term.

a. Generally accepted accounting principles
b. Net profit
c. Matching principle
d. Net income

15. In business and finance accounting, _____ is equal to the gross profit minus overheads minus interest payable plus/minus one off items for a given time period (usually: accounting period.)

Chapter 9. Financial Statements: The Scorecard 49

A common synonym for '_____' when discussing financial statements (which include a balance sheet and an income statement) is the bottom line. This term results from the traditional appearance of an income statement which shows all allocated revenues and expenses over a specified time period with the resulting summation on the bottom line of the report.

   a. Net profit
   b. Matching principle
   c. Generally accepted accounting principles
   d. Treasury stock

16. In economics, business, retail, and accounting, a _____ is the value of money that has been used up to produce something, and hence is not available for use anymore. In economics, a _____ is an alternative that is given up as a result of a decision. In business, the _____ may be one of acquisition, in which case the amount of money expended to acquire it is counted as _____.
   a. Cost overrun
   b. Cost
   c. Cost allocation
   d. Fixed costs

17. In financial accounting, _____ or cost of sales includes the direct costs attributable to the production of the goods sold by a company. This amount includes the materials cost used in creating the goods along with the direct labour costs used to produce the good. It excludes indirect expenses such as distribution costs and sales force costs.
   a. Reorder point
   b. 1990 Clean Air Act
   c. 28-hour day
   d. Cost of goods sold

18. _____, Gross profit margin or Gross Profit Rate can be defined as the amount of contribution to the business enterprise, after paying for direct-fixed and direct-variable unit costs, required to cover overheads (fixed commitments) and provide a buffer for unknown items. It expresses the relationship between gross profit and sales revenue.

It can be expressed in absolute terms:

Gross Profit = Revenue − Cost of Sales

or as the ratio of gross profit to sales revenue, usually in the form of a percentage:

_____ Percentage = (Revenue-Cost of Sales)/Revenue

Chapter 9. Financial Statements: The Scorecard

Cost of Sales includes variable costs and fixed costs directly linked to the product, such as material and labor.

a. 1990 Clean Air Act
b. Profit maximization
c. Gross margin
d. Profit margin

19. An _____, operating expenditure, operational expense, operational expenditure or OPEX is an on-going cost for running a product, business, or system. Its counterpart, a capital expenditure (CAPEX), is the cost of developing or providing non-consumable parts for the product or system. For example, the purchase of a photocopier is the CAPEX, and the annual paper and toner cost is the OPEX.

a. AAAI
b. A4e
c. A Stake in the Outcome
d. Operating expense

20. _____ is the difference between operating revenues and operating expenses, but it is also sometimes used as a synonym for EBIT and operating profit. This is true if the firm has no non-_____.

A professional investor contemplating a change to the capital structure of a firm first evaluates a firm's fundamental earnings potential (reflected by Earnings Before Interest, Taxes, Depreciation and Amortization EBITDA and EBIT), and then determines the optimal use of debt vs. equity.

a. AAAI
b. Operating income
c. A4e
d. A Stake in the Outcome

21. An _____ is a tax levied on the financial income of people, corporations, or other legal entities. Various _____ systems exist, with varying degrees of tax incidence. Income taxation can be progressive, proportional, or regressive.

a. A4e
b. A Stake in the Outcome
c. Ordinary income
d. Income tax

Chapter 9. Financial Statements: The Scorecard

22. An _____ is a practitioner of accountancy, which is the measurement, disclosure or provision of assurance about financial information that helps managers, investors, tax authorities and other decision makers make resource allocation decisions.

The word '_____' is derived from the French 'Compter' which took its origin from the Latin 'Computare'. The word was formerly written in English as 'Accomptant', but in process of time the word, which was always pronounced by dropping the 'p', became gradually changed both in pronunciation and in orthography to its present form.

   a. A Stake in the Outcome
   b. Accountant
   c. AAAI
   d. A4e

23. A _____ is a business that is privately owned and operated, with a small number of employees and relatively low volume of sales. The legal definition of 'small' often varies by country and industry, but is generally under 100 employees in the United States and under 50 employees in the European Union. In comparison, the definition of mid-sized business by the number of employees is generally under 500 in the U.S. and 250 for the European Union.

   a. Critical Success Factor
   b. Golden Boot Compensation
   c. Small Business
   d. Pre-determined overhead rate

Chapter 10. Financial Analysis: The Gauges

1. In financial accounting, a _____ or statement of financial position is a summary of a person's or organization's balances. Assets, liabilities and ownership equity are listed as of a specific date, such as the end of its financial year. A _____ is often described as a snapshot of a company's financial condition.
   a. Balance sheet
   b. 1990 Clean Air Act
   c. 33 Strategies of War
   d. 28-hour day

2. _____ refers to an assessment of the viability, stability and profitability of a business, sub-business or project.

   It is performed by professionals who prepare reports using ratios that make use of information taken from financial statements and other reports. These reports are usually presented to top management as one of their bases in making business decisions.

   a. 33 Strategies of War
   b. Financial analysis
   c. 1990 Clean Air Act
   d. 28-hour day

3. _____ are formal records of the financial activities of a business, person, or other entity. In British English, including United Kingdom company law, _____ are often referred to as accounts, although the term _____ is also used, particularly by accountants.

   _____ provide an overview of a business or person's financial condition in both short and long term.

   a. 1990 Clean Air Act
   b. 28-hour day
   c. 33 Strategies of War
   d. Financial statements

4. The _____ is a financial ratio that measures whether or not a firm has enough resources to pay its debts over the next 12 months. It compares a firm's current assets to its current liabilities. It is expressed as follows:

$$\text{Current ratio} = \frac{\text{Current Assets}}{\text{Current Liabilities}}$$

For example, if WXY Company's current assets are $50,000,000 and its current liabilities are $40,000,000, then its _____ would be $50,000,000 divided by $40,000,000, which equals 1.25.

Chapter 10. Financial Analysis: The Gauges

a. Times interest earned
b. Return on assets
c. Financial ratio
d. Current ratio

5. _____ is a financial metric which represents operating liquidity available to a business. Along with fixed assets such as plant and equipment, _____ is considered a part of operating capital. It is calculated as current assets minus current liabilities.

a. 33 Strategies of War
b. Working capital
c. 28-hour day
d. 1990 Clean Air Act

6. In finance, the _____ or quick ratio or liquid ratio measures the ability of a company to use its near cash or quick assets to immediately extinguish or retire its current liabilities. Quick assets include those current assets that presumably can be quickly converted to cash at close to their book values.

Generally, the acid test ratio should be 1:1 or better, however this varies widely by industry.

a. A Stake in the Outcome
b. A4e
c. Inventory turnover
d. Acid-test

7. _____ is a company's financial statement that indicates how the revenue is transformed into the net income The purpose of the _____ is to show managers and investors whether the company made or lost money during the period being reported.

The important thing to remember about an _____ is that it represents a period of time.

a. A Stake in the Outcome
b. A4e
c. AAAI
d. Income statement

Chapter 10. Financial Analysis: The Gauges

8. An _____, operating expenditure, operational expense, operational expenditure or OPEX is an on-going cost for running a product, business, or system. Its counterpart, a capital expenditure (CAPEX), is the cost of developing or providing non-consumable parts for the product or system. For example, the purchase of a photocopier is the CAPEX, and the annual paper and toner cost is the OPEX.
   a. Operating expense
   b. AAAI
   c. A Stake in the Outcome
   d. A4e

9. _____ is the difference between operating revenues and operating expenses, but it is also sometimes used as a synonym for EBIT and operating profit. This is true if the firm has no non-_____.

A professional investor contemplating a change to the capital structure of a firm first evaluates a firm's fundamental earnings potential (reflected by Earnings Before Interest, Taxes, Depreciation and Amortization EBITDA and EBIT), and then determines the optimal use of debt vs. equity.

   a. A Stake in the Outcome
   b. A4e
   c. AAAI
   d. Operating income

10. In a human resources context, _____ or labor _____ is the rate at which an employer gains and loses employees. Simple ways to describe it are 'how long employees tend to stay' or 'the rate of traffic through the revolving door.' _____ is measured for individual companies and for their industry as a whole. If an employer is said to have a high _____ relative to its competitors, it means that employees of that company have a shorter average tenure than those of other companies in the same industry.
   a. Turnover
   b. Career portfolios
   c. Ten year occupational employment projection
   d. Continuous

11. _____ is one of a series of accounting transactions dealing with the billing of customers who owe money to a person, company or organization for goods and services that have been provided to the customer. In most business entities this is typically done by generating an invoice and mailing or electronically delivering it to the customer, who in turn must pay it within an established timeframe called credit or payment terms.

An example of a common payment term is Net 30, meaning payment is due in the amount of the invoice 30 days from the date of invoice.

a. Accumulated Depreciation
b. Other revenue
c. A Stake in the Outcome
d. Accounts receivable

12. In finance, _____, is the ratio of money gained or lost on an investment relative to the amount of money invested. The amount of money gained or lost may be referred to as interest, profit/loss, gain/loss, or net income/loss. The money invested may be referred to as the asset, capital, principal, or the cost basis of the investment.
    a. Financial ratio
    b. Return on Capital Employed
    c. Return on sales
    d. Rate of return

13. In business and accounting, _____s are everything of value that is owned by a person or company. Any property or object of value that one possesses, usually considered as applicable to the payment of one's debts is considered an _____. Simplistically stated, _____s are things of value that can be readily converted into cash.
    a. A Stake in the Outcome
    b. A4e
    c. AAAI
    d. Asset

14. _____(requity)measures the rate of return on the ownership interest (shareholders' equity) of the common stock owners. It measures a firm's efficiency at generating profits from every dollar of shareholders' equity (also known as net assets or assets minus liabilities.) It shows how well a company uses investment dollars to generate earnings growth.
    a. Financial ratio
    b. Return on Capital Employed
    c. Rate of return
    d. Return on equity

15. _____ generally refers to a list of all planned expenses and revenues. It is a plan for saving and spending. A _____ is an important concept in microeconomics, which uses a _____ line to illustrate the trade-offs between two or more goods.
    a. Budget
    b. 33 Strategies of War
    c. 1990 Clean Air Act
    d. 28-hour day

16. _____ is one of the managerial functions like planning, organizing, staffing and directing. It is an important function because it helps to check the errors and to take the corrective action so that deviation from standards are minimized and stated goals of the organization are achieved in desired manner. According to modern concepts, _____ is a foreseeing action whereas earlier concept of _____ was used only when errors were detected. _____ in management means setting standards, measuring actual performance and taking corrective action.

a. Decision tree pruning
b. Control
c. Turnover
d. Schedule of reinforcement

Chapter 11. Human Resources: The People

1. _____ is the strategic and coherent approach to the management of an organisation's most valued assets - the people working there who individually and collectively contribute to the achievement of the objectives of the business. The terms '_____' and 'human resources' (HR) have largely replaced the term 'personnel management' as a description of the processes involved in managing people in organizations. In simple sense, _____ means employing people, developing their resources, utilizing, maintaining and compensating their services in tune with the job and organizational requirement.
    a. Job knowledge
    b. Revolving door syndrome
    c. Progressive discipline
    d. Human resource management

2. A _____ is a business that is privately owned and operated, with a small number of employees and relatively low volume of sales. The legal definition of 'small' often varies by country and industry, but is generally under 100 employees in the United States and under 50 employees in the European Union. In comparison, the definition of mid-sized business by the number of employees is generally under 500 in the U.S. and 250 for the European Union.
    a. Critical Success Factor
    b. Pre-determined overhead rate
    c. Golden Boot Compensation
    d. Small business

3. _____ is a contract between two parties, one being the employer and the other being the employee. An employee may be defined as: 'A person in the service of another under any contract of hire, express or implied, oral or written, where the employer has the power or right to control and direct the employee in the material details of how the work is to be performed.' Black's Law Dictionary page 471 (5th ed. 1979.)
    a. Employment rate
    b. Employment counsellor
    c. Exit interview
    d. Employment

4. The term _____ was created by President Lyndon B. Johnson when he signed Executive Order 11246 on September 24, 1965, created to prohibit federal contractors from discriminating against employees on the basis of race, sex, creed, religion, color, or national origin. In more recent times, most employers have also added sexual orientation to the list of non-discrimination.

The Executive Order also required contractors to implement affirmative action plans to increase the participation of minorities and women in the workplace.

a. Equal Employment Opportunity
   b. A4e
   c. A Stake in the Outcome
   d. AAAI

5. The U.S. _____ is a federal agency whose goal is ending employment discrimination. The _____ investigates discrimination complaints based on an individual's race, color, national origin, religion, sex, age, disability and retaliation for reporting and/or opposing a discriminatory practice. The Commission is also tasked with filing suits on behalf of alleged victim(s) of discrimination against employers and as an adjudicatory for claims of discrimination brought against federal agencies.
   a. Equal Employment Opportunity Commission
   b. Airbus Industrie
   c. ARCO
   d. Airbus SAS

6. _____ according to Onuoha (2007) is the practice of starting new organizations or revitalizing mature organizations, particularly new businesses generally in response to identified opportunities. _____ is often a difficult undertaking, as a vast majority of new businesses fail. Entrepreneurial activities are substantially different depending on the type of organization that is being started.
   a. A4e
   b. AAAI
   c. A Stake in the Outcome
   d. Entrepreneurship

7. An _____ is a person who has possession of an enterprise and assumes significant accountability for the inherent risks and the outcome. It is an ambitious leader who combines land, labor, and capital to create and market new goods or services. The term is a loanword from French and was first defined by the Irish economist Richard Cantillon.
   a. A4e
   b. AAAI
   c. Entrepreneur
   d. A Stake in the Outcome

8. _____ is unwelcome harassment of a sexual nature, or based upon the receiving party's sex or gender. In some contexts or circumstances, _____ may be illegal. It includes a range of behavior from seemingly mild transgressions and annoyances to actual sexual abuse or sexual assault.

a. 1990 Clean Air Act
b. 28-hour day
c. Hypernorms
d. Sexual harassment

9. _____ is a process for determining and addressing needs, or gaps between current conditions and desired conditions organizations it is known as community needs analysis. It involves identifying material problems/deficits/weaknesses and advantages/opportunites/strengths, and evaluating possible solutions that take those qualities into consideration.

a. 1990 Clean Air Act
b. Needs assessment
c. 28-hour day
d. 33 Strategies of War

10. _____ refers to the process of screening, and selecting qualified people for a job at an organization or firm mid- and large-size organizations and companies often retain professional recruiters or outsource some of the process to _____ agencies. External _____ is the process of attracting and selecting employees from outside the organization.

The _____ industry has four main types of agencies: employment agencies, _____ websites and job search engines, 'headhunters' for executive and professional _____, and in-house _____.

a. Referral recruitment
b. Recruitment
c. Labour hire
d. Recruitment Process Outsourcing

11. _____ is a form of communication that typically attempts to persuade potential customers to purchase or to consume more of a particular brand of product or service. 'While now central to the contemporary global economy and the reproduction of global production networks, it is only quite recently that _____ has been more than a marginal influence on patterns of sales and production. The formation of modern _____ was intimately bound up with the emergence of new forms of monopoly capitalism around the end of the 19th century and beginning of the 20th century as one element in corporate strategies to create, organize and where possible control markets, especially for mass produced consumer goods.

a. A Stake in the Outcome
b. A4e
c. AAAI
d. Advertising

Chapter 11. Human Resources: The People

12. A _____ is a quantitative research method commonly employed in survey research. The aim of this approach is to ensure that each interviewee is presented with exactly the same questions in the same order. This ensures that answers can be reliably aggregated and that comparisons can be made with confidence between sample subgroups or between different survey periods.

   a. Mystery shoppers
   b. Structured interview
   c. Questionnaire construction
   d. Questionnaire

13. A _____ is a formal statement of a set of business goals, the reasons why they are believed attainable, and the plan for reaching those goals. It may also contain background information about the organization or team attempting to reach those goals.

   The business goals may be defined for for-profit or for non-profit organizations.

   a. Time management
   b. Distributed management
   c. Business plan
   d. Crisis management

14. _____ is subcontracting a process, such as product design or manufacturing, to a third-party company. The decision to outsource is often made in the interest of lowering cost or making better use of time and energy costs, redirecting or conserving energy directed at the competencies of a particular business, or to make more efficient use of land, labor, capital, (information) technology and resources. _____ became part of the business lexicon during the 1980s.

   a. Unemployment insurance
   b. Opinion leadership
   c. Outsourcing
   d. Operant conditioning

15. _____ is a forward looking process for setting goals and regularly checking progress toward achieving those goals. It is a continual feedback process whereby the actual outputs are measured and compared with the desired goals. Any discrepancy or gap is then fed back into changing the inputs of the process, so as to achieve the desired goals or outputs.

   a. 28-hour day
   b. 33 Strategies of War
   c. 1990 Clean Air Act
   d. Performance management

Chapter 11. Human Resources: The People

16. _____ is an increasingly broadening term with which an organization, or other human system describes the combination of traditionally administrative personnel functions with acquisition and application of skills, knowledge and experience, Employee Relations and resource planning at various levels. The field draws upon concepts developed in Industrial/Organizational Psychology and System Theory. _____ has at least two related interpretations depending on context. The original usage derives from political economy and economics, where it was traditionally called labor, one of four factors of production although this perspective is changing as a function of new and ongoing research into more strategic approaches at national levels. This first usage is used more in terms of '_____ development', and can go beyond just organizations to the level of nations. The more traditional usage within corporations and businesses refers to the individuals within a firm or agency, and to the portion of the organization that deals with hiring, firing, training, and other personnel issues, typically referred to as `_____ management'.

   a. Bradford Factor
   b. Human resource management
   c. Progressive discipline
   d. Human resources

17. _____ is a method by which the job performance of an employee is evaluated _____ is a part of career development.

   _____s are regular reviews of employee performance within organizations

   Generally, the aims of a _____ are to:

   - Give feedback on performance to employees.
   - Identify employee training needs.
   - Document criteria used to allocate organizational rewards.
   - Form a basis for personnel decisions: salary increases, promotions, disciplinary actions, etc.
   - Provide the opportunity for organizational diagnosis and development.
   - Facilitate communication between employee and administraton
   - Validate selection techniques and human resource policies to meet federal Equal Employment Opportunity requirements.

   A common approach to assessing performance is to use a numerical or scalar rating system whereby managers are asked to score an individual against a number of objectives/attributes. In some companies, employees receive assessments from their manager, peers, subordinates and customers while also performing a self assessment.

   a. Personnel management
   b. Progressive discipline
   c. Performance appraisal
   d. Human resource management

18. A _____ is a set of categories designed to elicit information about a quantitative or a qualitative attribute. In the social sciences, common examples are the Likert scale and 1-10 _____s in which a person selects the number which is considered to reflect the perceived quality of a product.

A _____ is an instrument that requires the rater to assign the rated object that have numerals assigned to them.

a. Rating scale
b. Polytomous Rasch model
c. Spearman-Brown prediction formula
d. Thurstone scale

19. In human resources or industrial/organizational psychology, _____ ' 'multisource feedback,' or 'multisource assessment,' is feedback that comes from all around an employee. '360' refers to the 360 degrees in a circle, with an individual figuratively in the center of the circle. Feedback is provided by subordinates, peers, and supervisors.
a. Revolving door syndrome
b. Personnel management
c. 360-degree feedback
d. Job knowledge

20. _____ describes the situation when output from (or information about the result of) an event or phenomenon in the past will influence the same event/phenomenon in the present or future. When an event is part of a chain of cause-and-effect that forms a circuit or loop, then the event is said to 'feed back' into itself.

_____ is also a synonym for:

- _____ signal; the information about the initial event that is the basis for subsequent modification of the event.
- _____ loop; the causal path that leads from the initial generation of the _____ signal to the subsequent modification of the event.

_____ is a mechanism, process or signal that is looped back to control a system within itself. Such a loop is called a _____ loop.

a. Positive feedback
b. 1990 Clean Air Act
c. Feedback loop
d. Feedback

Chapter 11. Human Resources: The People

21. In economics and sociology, an _____ is any factor (financial or non-financial) that enables or motivates a particular course of action, or counts as a reason for preferring one choice to the alternatives. It is an expectation that encourages people to behave in a certain way. Since human beings are purposeful creatures, the study of _____ structures is central to the study of all economic activity (both in terms of individual decision-making and in terms of co-operation and competition within a larger institutional structure.)

   a. A4e
   b. A Stake in the Outcome
   c. AAAI
   d. Incentive

22. A _____ is a compensation, usually financial, received by a worker in exchange for their labor.

   Compensation in terms of _____s is given to worker and compensation in terms of salary is given to employees. Compensation is a monetary benefits given to employees in returns of the services provided by them.

   a. State Compensation Insurance Fund
   b. Performance-related pay
   c. Profit-sharing agreement
   d. Wage

23. In general, a _____ is an arrangement to provide people with an income when they are no longer earning a regular income from employment.

   The terms retirement plan or superannuation refer to a _____ granted upon retirement. Retirement plans may be set up by employers, insurance companies, the government or other institutions such as employer associations or trade unions.

   a. State Compensation Insurance Fund
   b. Pension
   c. Wage
   d. Pension insurance contract

24. _____ occurs when a person is available to work and seeking work but currently without work. The prevalence of _____ is usually measured using the _____ rate, which is defined as the percentage of those in the labor force who are unemployed. The _____ rate is also used in economic studies and economic indexes such as the United States' Conference Board's Index of Leading Indicators as a measure of the state of the macroeconomics.

Chapter 11. Human Resources: The People

a. Unemployment Convention, 1919
b. Employment-to-population ratio
c. Unemployment
d. Outplacement

25. _____ is money received by an unemployed worker from the United States or a state. In the United States, this compensation is classified as a type of social welfare benefit. According to the Internal Revenue Code, these types of benefits are to be included in a taxpayer's gross income.
a. Unemployment Provision Convention, 1934
b. Unemployment insurance
c. Unemployment
d. Unemployment compensation

26. An _____ details guidelines, expectations and procedures of a business or company to its employees.

_____s are given to employees on one of the first days of his/her job, in order to acquaint them with their new company and its policies.

Chapter 11. Human Resources: The People

While it often varies from business to business, specific areas that an _____ may address include:

- A welcome statement, which may also briefly describe the company's history, reasons for its success and how the employee can contribute to future successes. It may also include a mission statement, or a statement about a business' goals and objectives.
- Orientation procedures. This usually involves providing a human resources manager or other designated employee completed income tax withholding forms, providing proof of identity and eligibility for employment (in accordance with the Immigration Reform and Control Act of 1986), proof of a completed drug test (by a designated medical center) and other required forms.
- Definitions of full- and part-time employment, and benefits each classification receives. In addition, this area also describes timekeeping procedures (such as defining a 'work week'.) This area may also include information about daily breaks (for lunch and rest.)
- Information about employee pay and benefits (such as vacation and insurance.) Usually, new employees are awarded some benefits, plus additional rewards (such as enrollment in a 401K retirement account program, additional vacation and pay raises) after having worked for a company for a certain period of time. These are spelled out in this section.
- Expectations about conduct and discipline policies. These sections include conduct policies for such areas as sexual harassment, alcohol and drug use, and attendance; plus, grounds for dismissal (i.e., getting fired) and due process. This area may also include information about filing grievances with supervisors and/or co-workers, and communicating work-related issues with supervisors and/or company managers.
- Guidelines for employee performance reviews (such as how and when they are conducted.)
- Policies for promotion or demotion to a certain position.
- Rules concerning mail; use of the telephone, company equipment, Internet and e-mail; and employee use of motor vehicles for job assignments.
- Procedures on handling on-the-job accidents, such as those that result in injury.
- How an employee may voluntarily terminate his job (through retirement or resignation), and exit interviews.
- A requirement that employees keep certain business information confidential. This area usually includes information about releasing employee records and information, as well as who may retrieve and inspect the information.

If the employer is covered by the Family and Medical Leave Act of 1993 - generally 50 or more employees - a handbook must have information about FMLA.

New employees are usually required to sign a form stating they have read and understand the information, and accept the terms of the _____.

a. Informational interview
b. Employment
c. Employee handbook
d. Underemployment

27. _____ describes how content an individual is with his or her job.

The happier people are within their job, the more satisfied they are said to be. _____ is not the same as motivation, although it is clearly linked.

a. Goal-setting theory
b. Job satisfaction
c. Human relations
d. Job analysis

Chapter 12. Growing Ventures: The Future

1. A _____ is a business that is privately owned and operated, with a small number of employees and relatively low volume of sales. The legal definition of 'small' often varies by country and industry, but is generally under 100 employees in the United States and under 50 employees in the European Union. In comparison, the definition of mid-sized business by the number of employees is generally under 500 in the U.S. and 250 for the European Union.
   a. Critical Success Factor
   b. Pre-determined overhead rate
   c. Golden Boot Compensation
   d. Small business

2. An _____ is a person who has possession of an enterprise and assumes significant accountability for the inherent risks and the outcome. It is an ambitious leader who combines land, labor, and capital to create and market new goods or services. The term is a loanword from French and was first defined by the Irish economist Richard Cantillon.
   a. Entrepreneur
   b. A4e
   c. AAAI
   d. A Stake in the Outcome

3. _____ refers to a range of skills, tools, and techniques used to manage time when accomplishing specific tasks, projects and goals. This set encompass a wide scope of activities, and these include planning, allocating, setting goals, delegation, analysis of time spent, monitoring, organizing, scheduling, and prioritizing. Initially _____ referred to just business or work activities, but eventually the term broadened to include personal activities also.
   a. Voice of the customer
   b. Formula for Change
   c. Cash cow
   d. Time management

4. _____ is an all encompassing term within a broad spectrum of post-secondary learning activities and programs. The term is used mainly in the United States. Recognized forms of post-secondary learning activities within the domain include: degree credit courses by non-traditional students, non-degree career training, workforce training, formal personal enrichment courses (both on-campus and online) self-directed learning (such as through Internet interest groups, clubs or personal research activities) and experiential learning as applied to problem solving.
   a. 28-hour day
   b. 33 Strategies of War
   c. Continuing education
   d. 1990 Clean Air Act

Chapter 12. Growing Ventures: The Future

5. _____ is one of the managerial functions like planning, organizing, staffing and directing. It is an important function because it helps to check the errors and to take the corrective action so that deviation from standards are minimized and stated goals of the organization are achieved in desired manner. According to modern concepts, _____ is a foreseeing action whereas earlier concept of _____ was used only when errors were detected. _____ in management means setting standards, measuring actual performance and taking corrective action.

   a. Control
   b. Decision tree pruning
   c. Turnover
   d. Schedule of reinforcement

6. Engineering _____ is the permissible limit of variation in

   1. a physical dimension,
   2. a measured value or physical property of a material, manufactured object, system, or service,
   3. other measured values (such as temperature, humidity, etc.)
   4. in engineering and safety, a physical distance or space (_____), as in a truck (lorry), train or boat under a bridge as well as a train in a tunnel

   Dimensions, properties, or conditions may vary within certain practical limits without significantly affecting functioning of equipment or a process. _____s are specified to allow reasonable leeway for imperfections and inherent variability without compromising performance.

   The _____ may be specified as a factor or percentage of the nominal value, a maximum deviation from a nominal value, an explicit range of allowed values, be specified by a note or published standard with this information, or be implied by the numeric accuracy of the nominal value. _____ can be symmetrical, as in 40±0.1, or asymmetrical, such as 40+0.2/−0.1.

   a. Quality assurance
   b. Root cause analysis
   c. Zero defects
   d. Tolerance

7. _____ has been described as the 'process of social influence in which one person can enlist the aid and support of others in the accomplishment of a common task'. A definition more inclusive of followers comes from Alan Keith of Genentech who said '_____ is ultimately about creating a way for people to contribute to making something extraordinary happen.'

   _____ is one of the most salient aspects of the organizational context. However, defining _____ has been challenging.

a. 1990 Clean Air Act
b. Situational leadership
c. 28-hour day
d. Leadership

8. _____ is a forward looking process for setting goals and regularly checking progress toward achieving those goals. It is a continual feedback process whereby the actual outputs are measured and compared with the desired goals. Any discrepancy or gap is then fed back into changing the inputs of the process, so as to achieve the desired goals or outputs.
a. 28-hour day
b. 1990 Clean Air Act
c. 33 Strategies of War
d. Performance management

9. _____ is an effective method of monitoring a process through the use of control charts. Control charts enable the use of objective criteria for distinguishing background variation from events of significance based on statistical techniques. Much of its power lies in the ability to monitor both process center and its variation about that center.
a. Quality control
b. Single Minute Exchange of Die
c. Statistical process control
d. Process capability

10. _____ is an increasingly broadening term with which an organization, or other human system describes the combination of traditionally administrative personnel functions with acquisition and application of skills, knowledge and experience, Employee Relations and resource planning at various levels. The field draws upon concepts developed in Industrial/Organizational Psychology and System Theory. _____ has at least two related interpretations depending on context. The original usage derives from political economy and economics, where it was traditionally called labor, one of four factors of production although this perspective is changing as a function of new and ongoing research into more strategic approaches at national levels. This first usage is used more in terms of '_____ development', and can go beyond just organizations to the level of nations . The more traditional usage within corporations and businesses refers to the individuals within a firm or agency, and to the portion of the organization that deals with hiring, firing, training, and other personnel issues, typically referred to as `_____ management'.
a. Human resources
b. Progressive discipline
c. Bradford Factor
d. Human resource management

Chapter 12. Growing Ventures: The Future

11. In probability theory, a probability distribution is called _____ if its cumulative distribution function is _____. This is equivalent to saying that for random variables X with the distribution in question, Pr[X = a] = 0 for all real numbers a, i.e.: the probability that X attains the value a is zero, for any number a. If the distribution of X is _____ then X is called a _____ random variable.

   a. Decision tree pruning
   b. Pay Band
   c. Connectionist expert systems
   d. Continuous

12. _____ is a management process whereby delivery (customer valued) processes are constantly evaluated and improved in the light of their efficiency, effectiveness and flexibility.

   Some see it as a meta process for most management systems (Business Process Management, Quality Management, Project Management). Deming saw it as part of the 'system' whereby feedback from the process and customer were evaluated against organisational goals.

   a. First-mover advantage
   b. Continuous Improvement Process
   c. Critical Success Factor
   d. Sole proprietorship

13. _____ refers to increasing the spiritual, political, social or economic strength of individuals and communities. It often involves the empowered developing confidence in their own capacities.

   The term Human _____ covers a vast landscape of meanings, interpretations, definitions and disciplines ranging from psychology and philosophy to the highly commercialized Self-Help industry and Motivational sciences.

   a. Empowerment
   b. A Stake in the Outcome
   c. AAAI
   d. A4e

14. _____ is the change (processing) of information in any manner detectable by an observer. As such, it is a process which describes everything which happens (changes) in the universe, from the falling of a rock (a change in position) to the printing of a text file from a digital computer system. In the latter case, an information processor is changing the form of presentation of that text file.

Chapter 12. Growing Ventures: The Future

a. AAAI
b. A4e
c. A Stake in the Outcome
d. Information processing

15. _____ can be regarded as an outcome of mental processes (cognitive process) leading to the selection of a course of action among several alternatives. Every _____ process produces a final choice. The output can be an action or an opinion of choice.
    a. 28-hour day
    b. 1990 Clean Air Act
    c. Decision making
    d. 33 Strategies of War

16. _____ is exchange of capital, goods, and services across international borders or territories. In most countries, it represents a significant share of gross domestic product (GDP.) While _____ has been present throughout much of history, its economic, social, and political importance has been on the rise in recent centuries.
    a. A4e
    b. AAAI
    c. International trade
    d. A Stake in the Outcome

17. _____ is an integrated communications-based process through which individuals and communities discover that existing and newly-identified needs and wants may be satisfied by the products and services of others.

    _____ is defined by the American _____ Association as the activity, set of institutions, and processes for creating, communicating, delivering, and exchanging offerings that have value for customers, clients, partners, and society at large. The term developed from the original meaning which referred literally to going to market, as in shopping, or going to a market to buy or sell goods or services.

    a. Disruptive technology
    b. Market development
    c. Customer relationship management
    d. Marketing

18. Consumer market research is a form of applied sociology that concentrates on understanding the behaviours, whims and preferences, of consumers in a market-based economy, and aims to understand the effects and comparative success of marketing campaigns. The field of consumer _____ as a statistical science was pioneered by Arthur Nielsen with the founding of the ACNielsen Company in 1923.

Thus _____ is the systematic and objective identification, collection, analysis, and dissemination of information for the purpose of assisting management in decision making related to the identification and solution of problems and opportunities in marketing.

a. Marketing research
b. 1990 Clean Air Act
c. Marketing research process
d. Market analysis

19. _____ according to Onuoha (2007) is the practice of starting new organizations or revitalizing mature organizations, particularly new businesses generally in response to identified opportunities. _____ is often a difficult undertaking, as a vast majority of new businesses fail. Entrepreneurial activities are substantially different depending on the type of organization that is being started.

a. Entrepreneurship
b. A4e
c. AAAI
d. A Stake in the Outcome

20. In decision theory and estimation theory, the _____ of an estimator, $\hat{\theta}$, of an unknown parameter of the distribution, θ, is the expected value of the loss function

$$R(\theta, \hat{\theta}) = \mathbb{E}_\theta L(\theta, \hat{\theta}) = \int L(\theta, \hat{\theta})\, dP_\theta.$$

where dP_θ is a probability measure parametrized by θ.

- For a scalar parameter θ and a quadratic loss function,

$$L(\theta, \hat{\theta}) = (\theta - \hat{\theta})^2$$

the _____ function becomes the mean squared error of the estimate,

$$R(\theta, \hat{\theta}) = E_\theta(\theta - \hat{\theta})^2$$

- In density estimation, the unknown parameter is probability density itself. The loss function is typically chosen to be a norm in an appropriate function space. For example, for L^2 norm,

$$L(f, \hat{f}) = \|f - \hat{f}\|_2^2$$

the _____ function becomes the mean integrated squared error

$$R(f, \hat{f}) = E\|f - \hat{f}\|^2$$

a. Risk
b. Financial modeling
c. Linear model
d. Risk aversion

21. A _____ is a formal statement of a set of business goals, the reasons why they are believed attainable, and the plan for reaching those goals. It may also contain background information about the organization or team attempting to reach those goals.

The business goals may be defined for for-profit or for non-profit organizations.

a. Time management
b. Crisis management
c. Business plan
d. Distributed management

Chapter 12. Growing Ventures: The Future

22. _____ is the risk that the value of an investment will decrease due to moves in market factors. The four standard _____ factors are:

   - Equity risk, the risk that stock prices will change.
   - Interest rate risk, the risk that interest rates will change.
   - Currency risk, the risk that foreign exchange rates will change.
   - Commodity risk, the risk that commodity prices (e.g. grains, metals) will change.

   As with other forms of risk, _____ may be measured in a number of ways. Traditionally, this is done using a Value at Risk methodology. Value at risk is well established as a risk management technique, but it contains a number of limiting assumptions that constrain its accuracy.

   a. Taleb distribution
   b. Risk neutral
   c. 1990 Clean Air Act
   d. Market Risk

23. A _____ is a documented investigation of a Market that is used to inform a firm's planning activities particularly around decision of: inventory, purchase, work force expansion/contraction, facility expansion, purchases of capital equipment, promotional activities, and many other aspects of a company.

   Not all managers are asked to conduct a _____, but all managers must make decisions using _____ data and understand how the data was derived. So all managers need a reasonable understanding of the tools most used for making sales forecasts and analyzing markets.

   a. Marketing research
   b. 1990 Clean Air Act
   c. Marketing research process
   d. Market analysis

24. A _____ is a written document that details the necessary actions to achieve one or more marketing objectives. It can be for a product or service, a brand, or a product line. _____s cover between one and five years.
   a. Marketing strategy
   b. Disruptive technology
   c. Marketing plan
   d. Market development

25. In economics and especially in the theory of competition, _____ are obstacles in the path of a firm that make it difficult to enter a given market.

_____ are the source of a firm's pricing power - the ability of a firm to raise prices without losing all its customers.

The term refers to hindrances that an individual may face while trying to gain entrance into a profession or trade.

a. Predatory pricing
b. 28-hour day
c. 1990 Clean Air Act
d. Barriers to entry

26. A _____ is typically described as a deliberate plan of action to guide decisions and achieve rational outcome(s.) However, the term may also be used to denote what is actually done, even though it is unplanned.

The term may apply to government, private sector organizations and groups, and individuals.

a. 1990 Clean Air Act
b. Policy
c. 28-hour day
d. 33 Strategies of War

27. A niche market is the subset of the market on which a specific product is focusing on; Therefore the _____ defines the specific product features aimed at satisfying specific market needs, as well as the price range, production quality and the demographics that is intended to impact.

Every single product that is on sale can be defined by its niche market. As of special note, the products aimed at a wide demographics audience, with the resulting low price (due to Price elasticity of demand), are said to belong to the Mainstream niche, in practice referred only as Mainstream or of high demand.

a. Dominant logic
b. Prevailing wage
c. Market niche
d. Labor intensive

28. A _____ is a process that can allow an organization to concentrate its limited resources on the greatest opportunities to increase sales and achieve a sustainable competitive advantage. A _____ should be centered around the key concept that customer satisfaction is the main goal.

Chapter 12. Growing Ventures: The Future

A _____ is a written plan which combines product development, promotion, distribution, and pricing approach, identifies the firm's marketing goals, and explains how they will be achieved within a stated timeframe.

a. Product bundling
b. Disruptive technology
c. Category management
d. Marketing strategy

29. _____ are costs incurred on the purchase of land, buildings, construction and equipment to be used in the production of goods or the rendering of services. In other words, the total cost needed to bring a project to a commercially operable status. However, _____ are not limited to the initial construction of a factory or other business.

a. Capital costs
b. Fixed asset turnover
c. Contingent employment
d. Reservation wage

30. In economics, business, retail, and accounting, a _____ is the value of money that has been used up to produce something, and hence is not available for use anymore. In economics, a _____ is an alternative that is given up as a result of a decision. In business, the _____ may be one of acquisition, in which case the amount of money expended to acquire it is counted as _____.

a. Cost overrun
b. Fixed costs
c. Cost allocation
d. Cost

31. _____ is the state or fact of exclusive rights and control over property, which may be an object, land/real estate or intellectual property. An _____ right is also referred to as title. The concept of _____ has existed for thousands of years and in all cultures.

a. A4e
b. A Stake in the Outcome
c. Emanation of the state
d. Ownership

Chapter 12. Growing Ventures: The Future

32. Procter is a surname, and may also refer to:

    - Bryan Waller Procter (pseud. Barry Cornwall), English poet
    - Goodwin Procter, American law firm
    - _____, consumer products multinational

a. Strict liability
b. Downstream
c. Procter ' Gamble
d. Master and Servant Acts

ANSWER KEY

Chapter 1
1. a   2. a   3. d   4. d   5. a   6. d   7. b   8. d   9. a   10. d
11. a 12. d 13. b 14. c 15. d

Chapter 2
1. d   2. d   3. d   4. a   5. b   6. b   7. d   8. a   9. c   10. c
11. c 12. c 13. c 14. b 15. b 16. a 17. a

Chapter 3
1. d   2. d   3. d   4. c   5. a   6. d   7. d   8. c   9. d   10. d
11. a 12. a 13. d 14. d 15. d 16. d 17. b

Chapter 4
1. d   2. d   3. d   4. a   5. d   6. b   7. d   8. c   9. d

Chapter 5
1. d   2. d   3. a   4. b   5. d   6. d   7. d   8. d   9. d   10. b
11. c 12. a 13. c 14. d

Chapter 6
1. c   2. b   3. c   4. a   5. d   6. d   7. c   8. d   9. b   10. a
11. d 12. a 13. d 14. c 15. b 16. d 17. d 18. a 19. d 20. a
21. d 22. a

Chapter 7
1. d   2. a   3. d   4. d   5. c   6. d   7. d   8. d   9. d   10. b
11. a 12. d 13. d 14. d 15. b 16. d 17. d 18. d 19. a

Chapter 8
1. d   2. c   3. b   4. c   5. d   6. d   7. c   8. d   9. c   10. d
11. d 12. a 13. d 14. a 15. d 16. d 17. d 18. d 19. b 20. d
21. c 22. b 23. a

Chapter 9
1. a   2. d   3. d   4. c   5. d   6. d   7. a   8. a   9. c   10. b
11. d 12. d 13. d 14. d 15. a 16. b 17. d 18. c 19. d 20. b
21. d 22. b 23. c

Chapter 10
1. a   2. b   3. d   4. d   5. b   6. d   7. d   8. a   9. d   10. a
11. d 12. d 13. d 14. d 15. a 16. b

Chapter 11
1. d   2. d   3. d   4. a   5. a   6. d   7. c   8. d   9. b   10. b
11. d 12. b 13. c 14. c 15. d 16. d 17. c 18. a 19. c 20. d
21. d 22. d 23. b 24. c 25. d 26. c 27. b

ANSWER KEY

Chapter 12

1. d	2. a	3. d	4. c	5. a	6. d	7. d	8. d	9. c	10. a
11. d	12. b	13. a	14. d	15. c	16. c	17. d	18. a	19. a	20. a
21. c	22. d	23. d	24. c	25. d	26. b	27. c	28. d	29. a	30. d
31. d	32. c								

www.ingramcontent.com/pod-product-compliance
Lightning Source LLC
Chambersburg PA
CBHW081849230426
43669CB00018B/2875